WAR TORN SKIES

BEDFORDSHIRE

by

Paul Johnson

First published 2014.
Red Kite
PO Box 223,
Walton-on-Thames,
Surrey, KT12 3YQ
England
Tel. 0845 095 0346

© Paul Johnson 2013
All Rights Reserved.
No part of this publication
may be reproduced, stored
in any form of retrieval
system, or transmitted
in any form or by any
means without prior
permission in writing
from the publishers.

Series Editor Simon W Parry.
Design Amy Shore.

Printed by
Dimograf, Sp. Z o. o. Poland
Purchase this and other Red Kite books directly from Red Kite's websites;
www.redkitebooks.co.uk
www.wingleader.co.uk

First Edition
ISBN 978-906592-13-4

CONTENTS

Introduction	5
The Airfields	7
Map	19

The Golden Years
The First to Fall	20
Mid-Air Collision over Henlow	24
An Acrobat Dies over Clifton	27
Flying Duchess Loses Private Pilot at Lidlington	31
A Tiger on Dunstable Downs	36
First Loss at Cranfield	38
The Battle of Carlton	40

1940
The George Cross is Won at Cranfield	41
A Fiery Comet Falls rrom the Dark Skies (by Julian Evan-Hart)	45
Local Lad Flies into Tree at Turvey	48
Rare Reconnaissance Type at Eaton Socon (by Julian Evan-Hart)	52

1941
Bale Out over Husband Crawley	58
Death of a Bedford Schoolboy	60
Christmas Eve Crash in Kempston	63

1942
The Desert Air Force Collide over Bedford	66

1943
Two Night-fighters in Two Nights	69
Thunderbolts over Eaton Ford	72
An Unusual Bird at Whipsnade	74
Black Thursday - A Hells Angel in the Garden	76
Remembrance Day Collision over Cranfield	86
Lightning Strikes Twice and Pilot Survives	90

1944
Mystery at Tetworth Hall - The Perils of Internet Research	91
A Thunderbolt Strikes at Podington	96
A Tradegy at Yeldon	98
A Raider Strikes at Little Staughton	104
The Piggyback Ride over Eaton Socon	106
Mission 512 – The Death of 'Miss Liberty Belle'	108
Bravery over Potton	114
Death Rains Down on Thurleigh	117

1945
An Eagle Lands in Biggleswade	122
Valentine's Day Disaster over Sandy	124
A Belgian Dies at Flitwick	128
Anniversary Loss – A P-47 at Astwood	129

And Still They Fell – Accidents Post WW2
A Tempest Strikes Meppershall	131
The Potton Wood Liberator	134
The Cranfield Victor	137

Bombs & Rockets In Bedfordshire
Raiders at Vauxhall	140
Lone Raiders	145
The Vengeance Weapons	148
Whispering Death – A V-2 Strikes Without Warning	150

Bedfordshire Incident & Accident Log	154
Sources of Information	159
References	160

INTRODUCTION

I have been involved in military and aviation research for over 30 years. This publication is the result of a desire to share with the world some of the facts about aircraft accidents and losses in the UK prior to, and throughout, the Second World War. Since the early days of flight Bedfordshire has witnessed many milestones in aviation history as technological advances were made in both the aircraft and airship industries. Names such as Cranfield and Cardington became renowned for their part in the development of many types of air transport over the years, much of which was used for military purposes. The onset of the Second World War saw a massive increase in aircraft development as well as in the needs of the Royal Air Force, as pilots and aircrew undertook numerous training, conversion and operational flights. During the early stages of the war the rapid expansion of the aircrew training programme brought with it an unfortunate increase in the number of aviation accidents. Many of these crash sites have been lost to the tide of time and those who witnessed these incidents become fewer with each passing year. As the war progressed, Bedfordshire saw the creation of a series of new airfields from which recently formed units would operate and, as a result, aircraft accidents increased still further. A tour across the county today can, in some cases, bring you face to face with some of these remnants of Britain's air war. Some have been converted to use by light industry and bring prosperity to the towns and villages that once hosted the uniformed hordes of Allied airmen and women. Others have returned to the agricultural land from which they were born. A few have remained exactly as they were left after passing from military use and lie, derelict and decaying, hidden in the fields and woodlands of the county where they were once so active.

The arrival of the United States Army Air Force in 1942 significantly increased the level of air traffic across Bedfordshire's airfields as the Americans also carried out training flights and operational missions. Inevitably, this escalating level of flights led to a considerable number of accidents which had both tragic and, in some cases, miraculous outcomes. There are many stories of how battle weary aircraft, often with wounded men aboard, managed to reach the 'home field' only to suffer traumatic engine failure and crash to earth, just a few hundred yards from safety. Others were involved in tragic mid-air collisions or incidents where the heavily laden aircraft became uncontrollable shortly after leaving the ground. In these cases there was nearly always significant loss of life, both for those aboard the aircraft as well as those on the ground.

For the civilian population there was also death and danger from the skies, not only due to the fact that they were often in the path of many accidents but that they were also subjected to air raids and attacks brought about by the continuing improvements in enemy weapons technology. I have attempted to cover some of the major incidents that affected the men, women and children of the towns and villages across Bedfordshire, as well those occasions where there their efforts to save the crew of stricken aircraft resulted in an award for bravery. The scope of this book is not intended to be a comprehensive representation of everything that happened concerning aviation history in the county, as this would result in a gargantuan tome. I have had to be selective concerning the topics covered, although each incident in itself is unique and reflective of a certain period. There are some areas of minimal detail and where these occur it is most likely due to them having already been covered adequately in other publications, such as particular airfield histories; some subjects may be touched on lightly, whilst others are in themselves highly detailed accounts. Like all books in this series one of the main aims is to ensure that the less publicised events are not lost to history, whilst another is to stimulate interest in certain subjects that may hopefully lead the reader to conduct a personal, much greater detailed research of their own. The author hopes that some of the contents of this volume will be accepted and considered as a very small but important step to prevent the loss of these aspects to our countries aviation history. Concerning research, I would at this stage like to mention that many areas of the text and the crash listings at the end of the volume were produced with reference to official documentation of the period and this, in itself, often contains omissions and errors. I have made every effort, to correct these and ensure that historical accuracy is maintained. It is my hope that I have made some small contribution to retaining Britain's aviation history as well as honouring those who have lost their lives in aircraft accidents in the county.

THE AIRFIELDS

Cardington

Cardington holds a special place in British aviation history because of its association with the H.M. Airship R101, and the terrible disaster that befell her crew and passengers on 5th October 1930. The site was originally built for the Shorts Airship Construction Company, where the R31 and R32 were built, and the huge airship sheds were later used to build the R101. The site faced closure following the R101 disaster but was saved when it was decided to re-establish the barrage balloon defence system throughout the UK. No.1 Balloon Training Unit was formed at Cardington on 9th January 1937 and a month later the first Barrage Balloon Group, No 30, was formed there. In September 1937 No.2 RAF Recruitment Centre moved in from Henlow and was soon followed by the Aircrew Selection and Medical Boards. In November 1938, No.30 Group became Balloon Command and by September 1939 almost fifty balloon squadrons had been formed, manning about 600 sites across the country. In November 1943 No.1 Balloon Training Unit was closed, having seen some 22,000 operators and drivers through its courses. Balloon Command was disbanded in February 1945. After the war Cardington was to also house No.102 Personnel Despatch Centre so many of those who had joined the RAF here passed through its gates again as they were demobilised. The large airship hangars still linger on as a reminder of the site's once thriving past. The Airship Heritage Trust national headquarters is at RAF Cardington, in a building beside the hangars. The RAF maintain a reserve collection of aircraft and a restoration centre at Cardington for the museums at Hendon and Cosford. The former RAF station premises at Shortstown has spent many years in a decaying state but is now in the process of rejuvenation, soon to become the site of a series of luxury apartments and dwellings.

Above: The large airship hangars at Cardington.

Cranfield

The airfield opened in June 1937 and a month later it came under the control of No.1 Group, Bomber Command. In the first week of July the sound of the Hawker Hind aircraft of Nos. 62, 82 and 108 Squadrons could be heard as they arrived at the newly laid site. When No.6 Group, Bomber Command, was formed in April 1937 it moved to Cranfield. In the early months of 1938 No. 62 and 82 Squadrons were re-equipped with Blenheims and in July of that year, the station was transferred to No.2 Group, Bomber Command. From August 1939, No.35 and 207 Squadrons, flying Fairey Battles, used the airfield for training pilots and observer/air gunners. In the winter of 1939/40 the runways at Cranfield were upgraded and by the spring of 1940 it was a prime RAF station with excellent facilities and three tarmac runways. No.51 Operational Training Unit arrived during the first week of August 1941 from Debden to train night fighter crews on Havocs, Blenheims and, later, Beaufighters and Mosquitos. In August 1942 the unit began training USAAF crews and in April 1943 it was transferred to No. 9 Group, Bomber Command with the unit finally disbanding on 14th June 1945. After the war Cranfield briefly served as a base for the repatriation of Canadian and

Australian airmen. In 1946 it became home to the Empire Test Pilots' School who moved in from Boscombe Down and, also, the College of Aeronautics. The ETPS subsequently moved to Farnborough in August 1947 and the location became known as Cranfield College of Technology. In 1969, the College of Technology received University status. The site today is a thriving example of the growth, development and rejuvenation of a military airfield into a place of significant academic achievement.

Gransden Lodge

Gransden Lodge opened early in 1942 as a satellite to Tempsford airfield. No.1418 (Experimental) Flight were the first to arrive to perform work on a number of electronic devices. The Wireless Investigation Flight, detached from 109 Squadron, arrived on 4th July 1942, later becoming 1474 Flight. Both units flew Wellingtons, the former conducting trials of Gee, the navigation aid. No.1474 Flight became No.192 Squadron on 4th January 1943, shortly after receiving Wellington Xs and a few Mosquito IVs. No. 1418 Flight conducted various trials with bombers and on 20th July 1942 was absorbed by the Bombing Development Unit. This unit and No.192 Squadron moved to Feltwell early in April 1943. No.1517 BAT Flight also used Gransden in 1943. The station became fully operational as part of No.8 Group providing training as the Pathfinder Navigation Training Unit equipped with Halifax IIs. This unit moved to Upwood and Warboys in June 1943 in order that the Canadian unit, No.405 (Vancouver) Squadron, could make Gransden Lodge its home for the remainder of the war. They had arrived from Leeming in Yorkshire on 19th April 1943 and eighteen months later, on 27th August 1944, No.142 Squadron arrived with their Mosquitos and were engaging the enemy the following day with the first of their operations. It flew 1,221 sorties during 169 operations - 61 of them against Berlin - and lost only two aircraft. Another three were destroyed in crashes and two written off after battle damage. A typical wartime station, well dispersed and unusually set away from roads and amidst fields, it had the customary three runways, one of 2,000yards and two of 1,400yards. There were two 'T2' hangars and a 'B1', along with 36 hardstandings. Gransden was a smaller station than many, with accommodation for 86 officers, nearly 200 NCOs and over 800 airmen. Quarters were also available for nearly 300 WAAFS. No.692 Squadron armed with Mosquito B.16s moved in on 4th June 1945 when the Canadians left Gransden Lodge. The Mosquitos of No.142 and 692 Squadrons were disbanded in September 1945. Transport Command took over the station for a short while in December 1945, with the Liberators of No.53 Squadron. The squadron disbanded on the 1st March 1946. The station's main runway was maintained into the 1950s for emergency use and also because Gransden had been earmarked for possible development into a permanent bomber station. Today, Little Gransden, as it is now known, is the base of the Cambridge Gliding Centre.

Henlow

Henlow was chosen as a military aircraft repair depot in 1917. Much of the station was still under construction when the Royal Flying Corps formally became the Royal Air Force on 1st April 1918. RAF Henlow started life as an Aircraft Repair Depot on 10th May 1918 and now boasts over 90 years of continuous service. The Station Operational Record Book (ORB) on that day states: -"A draft of approximately 40 airmen of various trades came from Farnborough under the command of Lt Col Stapleton-Cotton to form the depot. The men were of various trades. In the first few months the men were engaged in making shop equipment, trestles and benches in whatever workshops they visited, for the camp was still in the hands of the builders, who employed many Irishmen, who were almost foreigners, in speech, habits etc, and were housed in wooden huts where 194 shed now is." In the original and first list of RAF stations for April 1918, Henlow counts among only seven other stations which remain open as Royal Air Force stations today: -Halton, Leuchars, Northolt, Uxbridge, Waddington, and Wyton. On 1st April 1919, when the RAF was only a year old, about 100 airmen who were awaiting demobilisation were involved in a mutiny at Henlow. Dissatisfaction arose because of an increase in working hours as a result of the introduction of British Summer Time. Loyal airmen and NCOs rounded up the mutineers whilst the remainder of the depot were sent on a route march. Fifty-six people were tried by Courts-Martial in the weeks following the mutiny and severe jail sentences awarded. On 20th September 1925 the Parachute Test Unit (PTU), which was a detachment from the Air Ministry, was established at Henlow. One tragic accident that occurred during

Below:
The remains of an airfield defence post at Henlow.

the PTU's existence was on 9th March 1927. Corporal Arthur East jumped from an aircraft over RAF Biggin Hill at a height of 6,200 feet and carried out a delayed drop of over 5,000 feet in an attempt to beat the world 'delayed drop' record of 4,300 feet, then held by the Americans. It had been the intention to land in a valley but, unfortunately, he drifted over high ground and with his chute only half deployed he was killed instantly. Two days later LAC Dobbs, nicknamed 'Brainy' because of his many eccentric flying experiments, was using a balloon to jump over low hedges and trees when he hit an 11,000 Volt conductor carrying electricity from Willesden to Hendon and was also killed. It is said that his ghost still haunts the station and on cold and windy nights it can be heard walking through the hangars. It was also 'Brainy', who used to tie his dog to a suitable harness and miniature parachute, then drop the animal from the roof to study the parachute's behaviour. Prior to WW2 the site provided a variety of training and development courses in the RAF Technical College. In April 1938 Maintenance Command was formed and the unit at Henlow became No.13 Maintenance Unit under the control of No.43 Group, mainly for repair and modification of aircraft. In January 1940 the first Canadian built Hurricane aircraft arrived at Henlow for assembly, test and delivery to the operational squadrons. By June 1940 most of the training units had left the station. The Nazi Command clearly considered Henlow to be of some strategic importance as it was bombed by the Luftwaffe in September and November 1940, February 1941 and July 1942 without serious damage, although some casualties were sustained. In the winter of 1944 a V-1 'Doodlebug' and two V-2s also fell in the vicinity of the airfield, but it suffered very little damage and no casualties, other than a lost tooth. At the end of 1944 No.13 MU was still the main occupant at Henlow but No.6 Repairable Equipment Unit (REU) was also based there, as well as a number of mobile dental units and the School of Aeronautical Engineering. Today the main occupant is the RAF Radio Engineering Unit.

Little Staughton

The airfield was built in 1942, as a standard bomber station. It was only to exist for less than three years but saw plenty of action as AAF Station 127, a repair base for damaged American B-17s. Little Staughton remained a maintenance depot until February 1944 when it became a Pathfinder station. No.582 Squadron was officially formed at the airfield on 1st April 1944 and was joined the next day by the Mosquito crews of No.109 Squadron from Marham. The squadron saw action over Cologne only three days later and many more sorties were soon to be flown by them. The Lancasters went

*Above:
A 582 Squadron Lancaster being bombed up at Little Staughton.*

into action on the 9th and took part in many intensive raids in France and Belgium. Both squadrons were very active on 5th/6th June, the eve of D-Day, and continued afterwards with many successful and heroic missions. One Mosquito XVI, crewed by Flying Officers A.C. Austin and P. Moorehead dropped the last bombs of the war at 02:14 hours on 21st April 1945. At the end of 1945 the airfield was placed under care and maintenance but was effectively closed to service flying and is now in very limited use by a small number of private aircraft. Outside of the airfield gates can be found a small memorial to those men of the Pathfinder Squadrons who operated from the airfield at the height of its existence.

Luton

The airfield was originally started by private aviators and was first put to commercial use in 1932. It was officially opened on the 16th July 1938 by the Right Honourable Kingsley Wood, Secretary of State for Air, as London Luton Airport. Later that year the Elementary & Reserve Flying Training School opened its doors but at the outbreak of war all civilian flying ceased and the school closed. Training returned to Luton on 22nd July 1940 when No.24 Elementary Flying Training School moved there.

The unit moved to Sealand in Cheshire in February 1942 and was replaced in April by No.5 Ferry Pool of the Air Transport Auxiliary (ATA), the only all female pool, which moved to Luton from nearby Hatfield. The airfield was a base for No.264 Fighter Squadron as well as a manufacturing facility for the production of Percival Proctors and Airspeed Oxfords. By 1943 the ATA had more than 600 pilots and late in the year moved on to Cosford to allow room for Mosquito manufacture. In May 1944 Winston Churchill praised the fact that, under the command of Air Commodore D'Erlanger, more than 200,000 aircraft ferry flights had been undertaken since 1940 on behalf of the RAF and Royal Navy, whilst expressing regret at the loss of 113 pilots. The ATA disbanded at the end of November 1945. In 1952, civil use of the airport resumed and a new control tower was opened. The airport has developed since the late 1950s into a major international passenger airport.

Milton Ernest Hall

Originally designed by William Butterfield as a family home for the Starey family, Milton Ernest Hall is surrounded in intrigue and rumour. The onset of the Second World War saw the hall used for military purposes concerned with secret Allied radio and propaganda transmissions, political warfare, and undercover operations by British and American units. In 1944 it was officially the 8th Air Force Service Command HQ and Glenn Miller often stayed there, along with his manager, Don Haynes. The US Army Air Force Band used the hall for its meals in between broadcasts and rehearsals in Bedford and, in return for the hospitality shown by General Goodrich and his officers, Glenn Miller agreed to play a concert in the grounds of the hall on the afternoon of 16th July 1944, which was a huge success with over 1,600 officers and men present. It was from the hall that the famous band leader left for his fatal flight from nearby Twinwoods airfield. Today the hall is a residential home but little has changed to its exterior and it is easy to imagine the courtyard filled with the uniformed men and women of the Allied forces as they passed through its doors.

Podington

Podington was originally built as an RAF Bomber Command Station. On 19th April 1942 it transferred to the 8th USAAF. The first USAAF unit to use the airfield was the 28th Troop Carrier Squadron who arrived in June 1942 from Westover Army Air Field, Massachusetts. The 28th TCS flew Douglas C-47s from the base until moving to RAF Aldermaston in August 1942. Several units used it as a temporary base before the airfield was improved and runways extended, with the 8th Bomber Command Combat Crew Replacement Unit being stationed at the base between August 1942 and May 1943. On the 30th April 1942 the 100th Bomb Group moved to Podington from Thorpe Abbotts, and stayed there until the 8th June 1943. On 11th September 1943 the 92nd Bomb Group nicknamed 'Fames Favoured Few' moved to Podington from Alconbury with its B-17s and remained at the station until July 1945. The group flew over 300 missions from the airfield with the loss of 154 aircraft and crews in combat. It is credited with leading the 8th Air Force mission of 14th October 1943 to Schweinfurt, known as Black Thursday, and the mission of 25th April 1945 to Pilsen, Czechoslovakia, the last bombing mission by the 8th Air Force in Europe. Podington, which is one of the better preserved wartime airfields, is now better known as Santa Pod, the major European centre for drag racing. The old control tower is one of the few to have been converted into an unusual private house.

Tempsford

Construction began on Tempsford Flats in July 1940 and the completed airfield was handed over to No.3 Group RAF, responsible for Special Duty Operations, in October 1941. In December of that year the Wellingtons of No.11 Operational Training Unit were stationed at the airfield whilst their base at Bassingbourn was being improved. In January 1942 the HQ and Wireless Development Flights of No.109 Squadron moved in to begin trials with OBOE, the radio direction finding equipment, and other secret radio equipment. No.138 (Special Duty) Squadron moved into Tempsford in March 1942, together with their Whitley and Lysander aircraft to carry out covert supply and agent delivery operations. In the same month secure communications were established with SOE (Special Operations Executive)

A 138 Squadron Stirling stands near the control tower at RAF Tempsford.

and SIS (Secret Intelligence Service) sections in Baker Street, London. The container packing facilities and agent holding centre was set up at Gaynes Hall, near St Neots and Hazells Hall, near the airfield on the road to Sandy, was requisitioned for staff and agent accommodation. The first covert supply mission was carried out to a drop zone in northern France on 18th March 1942. On 10th April No.161 (Special Duties) Squadron moved into the airfield from Graveley, and took over dispersal areas on the western side of the airfield. The newly formed squadron was engaged in the skilled duties of landing and picking-up 'passengers' behind enemy lines using Lysander aircraft. At the same time, Handley Page Halifax IIs, specially modified for SOE operations, were delivered to No.138 Squadron. These aircraft are able to carry 15 containers and began to replace the ageing Whitley aircraft that had been used up until this point. On 20th April 1942 the buildings of Gibraltar Farm, on the eastern perimeter of the airfield were converted into high security SOE stores. The farmhouse was developed into an agent reception and pre-flight preparation centre and was to be the last place that many SOE operatives were to pass through. In February 1943 the first Lockheed Hudsons were taken on charge for pick-up operations, giving an increased capacity over the Lysanders and in October the first double Hudson pick up, flown by Wing Commander Hodges, brought back 10 personnel, including Monsieur Vincent Auriol, who later became President of France. On 25th October 1943 the US fledgling Special Duty Unit, the USAAF 801st (Provisional) Bomb Group, moved into the base for training and flew 'buddy missions' in Halifax aircraft prior to eventually moving into Harrington, where they become known as the 'Carpetbaggers', flying four squadrons of B-24 Liberator aircraft on covert supply missions. Sadly, the first Hudson to be lost on operations was shot down over Tilburg in Holland on the 31st May 1944, just as pick-up operations began to increase prior to the D-Day period. Although there were three pick-ups during the period between 2nd-7th June, there were no others until 3rd/4th July. One of the most famous drops was on the night of 7th/8th June 1944 when Violet Szabo along with three other agents were flown from Tempsford in a US 'Carpetbagger' B24 Liberator. No.138 Squadron converted to Short Stirling Mk IV aircraft in August 1944, giving more capacity for stores. These aircraft were able to carry 20 containers compared with the Halifax's 15. In the autumn of 1944 No.138 Squadron began to increase its operations to supply Norwegian Resistance. These missions proved hazardous owing to difficult terrain and bad weather. As the Allies advanced across Europe the distance to drop zones increased and operations to the low countries and south-west France became the main destinations. In March 1945 Tempsford came under control of No.38 Group and in April No.138 Squadron departed for RAF Tuddenham, to convert to Lancaster bombers. During operations from Tempsford the squadron had flown 29,000 containers, 10,000 packages and 995 agents in, and as many personnel out, of Europe. Seventy aircraft were lost, most crews being killed. No.161 Squadron continued operations until hostilities ceased on 7th May and the squadron was disbanded on 2nd June having made 1,749 sorties with the loss of 49 aircraft. Tempsford was taken over on 20th June 1945 by No.426 Squadron who used B-24 Liberators to bring back servicemen from Europe and India. Their trooping work completed, No.426 Squadron was disbanded in December 1945 and the B-24s were flown to Gransden Lodge. After a period of little activity RAF Maintenance took over the airfield on 7th August 1946 and various small detachments came and went. In the spring of 1947 Harvards and Mosquitos were briefly based at the airfield but in the autumn Tempsford was transferred to a care and maintenance state. In February 1963 many of the buildings were sold and the site reverted to the original owners. Today there is very little left of the original airfield but the barn through which so many SOE agents passed serves as a memorial to the site, to the bravery of the men and women who served there.

Thurleigh

The airfield was built in 1941 and on 7th September 1942 the first contingent of the 306th Bomb Group, United States Army Air Force started to arrive, with some of their B-17s flying in during the following week. From 9th October the 306th Bomb Group, nicknamed 'The Reich Wreckers',

Above:
The construction of roads and perimeter tracks continued at Thurleigh well into 1942.

mounted a long, arduous and very costly offensive from the station. The Group Commander, Colonel Overacker, led the first daylight precision attack against locomotive works at Lille, France, and by 19th April 1945 had reached at total of 342 missions, the second highest for any B-17 Group. During its time at Thurleigh over 9,600 sorties had been flown with the loss of 171 aircraft in action and over 22,500 tons of bombs were dropped. Sgt Maynard H. Smith won the Medal of Honor for his performance on 1st May 1943, when the aircraft on which he was a gunner was hit and caught fire in the radio compartment and waist sections. The sergeant threw exploding ammunition overboard, manned a gun until the German fighters were driven off, administered first aid to a wounded gunner, and extinguished the fire. In 1946 construction work began on the airfield to turn the site into what is now know as the Royal Aeronautical Establishment, Bedford. The airfield was finally closed in 1997 with the RAE becoming the Defence Evaluation and Research Agency and moving its experimental operations to Boscombe Down. With the end of military control, the airfield has been divided into two parts. The southern part is now known as Thurleigh Business Park, and includes the runway, which is currently used for the mass storage of new cars, although it remains intact for possible future use. The northern part houses the Bedford Autodrome, as well as 306th Bombardment Group Museum. A memorial to the 306th Bomb Group can be found along the Keysoe Road leading from the village of Thurleigh.

Twinwood Farm

The RAF had been using the grassed field as a landing ground for the Oxfords of No.14 Service Flying Training School from Cranfield until August 1941 when No.51 Operational Training Unit was formed. Twinwoods, as it was generally known, was used for the training of night fighter crews. By April 1942 it had been given a major facelift having three concrete runways and additional temporary buildings added. No.51 OTU remained at Twinwoods until the end of hostilities training aircrew on the use of Blenheim, Beaufighter and Mosquito aircraft. The United States Army Air Force Band, led by Glenn Miller, arrived in the Spring of 1944 and established an association with the airfield as it used it to fly to and from some of the more distant venues on their exhausting tour. In recognition of the services the airfield provided the band gave a concert at the airfield on 27th August 1944. It was from this station that Glenn Miller made his last flight on the 15th December 1944. The airfield closed in June 1945 and returned to agricultural use. The old control tower was purchased privately in 1999 and now houses the Twinwood Aviation Museum. The Glenn Miller Museum can be found in a section of the old flight office building, which was once used as a lecture room. The airfield has become a mecca for swing dance enthusiasts and living history re-enactors as it hosts the annual Glenn Miller Festival.

Woburn Park

The airstrip, which ran uphill to the west of the Abbey from the lake at the south end of the park, was originally built for Mary the Duchess of Bedford in the 1930s. Dame Mary died in 1937, aged 71, after leaving Woburn Abbey in a de Havilland Gipsy Moth to view the flooded Cambridgeshire Fens and complete her 200 hours of solo flying. She never returned and a search did not find her. However, some parts of her aircraft were found eventually having been washed ashore near Great Yarmouth but her body was never recovered. The airstrip was commandeered by the RAF in the Second World War and was known as No.34 Satellite Landing Ground. In 1941 Spitfires were housed there, later followed by Halifaxes, Stirlings and the odd Lancaster.

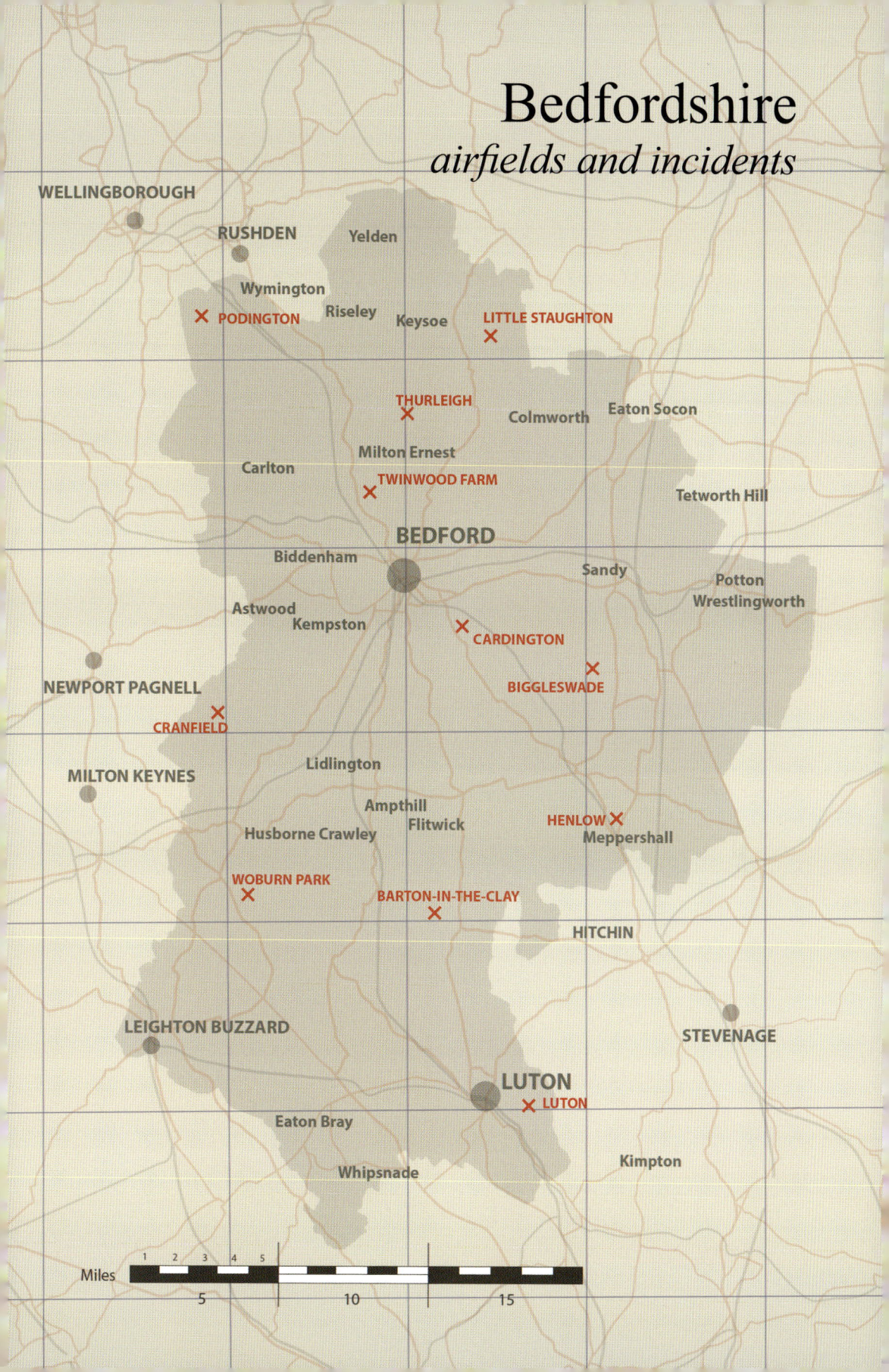

Bedfordshire
airfields and incidents

THE GOLDEN YEARS

THE FIRST TO FALL

One of the first incidents recorded by the Accident Investigation Branch in Bedfordshire was on the evening of Monday 16th August 1920 when a young pilot, James Gordon Riley, was at the controls of an Armstrong Whitworth F.K.8 (G-EALW). The aircraft had been giving pleasure flights during July 1920 when it made a forced landing in a corn field near Biddenham after the engine failed, due to a broken valve. During the landing the aircraft had suffered a damaged undercarriage and, as a result, could not be removed until the wheat crop had been cut. Whilst awaiting removal from the field the damaged undercarriage was replaced by mechanics from RAF Henlow and was soon ready for recovery.

The pilot was born in Maxwell Terrace, Thornliebank, Glasgow on 19th June 1899, the son of Joshua and Annie Riley. Whilst still a student he had applied for service in the Royal Flying Corps and, on 28th March 1918, joined No.70 Squadron in the field at Marieux, France.

16th August 1920

LOCATION
Biddenham

TYPE
Armstrong Whitworth F.K.8

SERIAL No.
G-EALW

PILOT
James Gordon RILEY
aged 21 - killed

CREW
Corporal H E HAMBLIN
injured

He went on to serve with the RAF in France and Egypt and had considerable experience on both F.E.2b and Handley Page aircraft but had only ever flown the Armstrong Whitworth aircraft on one previous occasion, which was the day of the forced landing. He had been demobilised from the RAF on 29th April 1920 and had been granted his civil pilot's licence (No.530b) on 20th June that year. At that time he was living at 'Thornlee', Oak Tree Drive, Palmers Green in North London. He later became a shareholder and pilot in the By-Air Company who had purchased the aircraft from the Disposal Board in September 1919. The objective was to present members of the public with a chance to ride in a flying machine for a small but profitable fee that offered both the excitement, and potential danger, of the early days of flight.

Above: An Armstrong Whitworth F.K.8 photographed during wartime military service.

On 13th August Corporal Hamblin, who was on leave from his job as an RAF mechanic, was engaged by the company as a ground engineer. He had served with the Army Cyclist Corps and the Royal Flying Corps during WW1 and had seen service on the Western Front since December 1915.

Hamblin carried out repairs and servicing on the F.K.8 on 14th August, including cleaning the spark plugs. The following morning the petrol, oil and water tanks were filled by both Hamblin and James Riley, who then carried out a ground test by starting the engine and revving it up to about 1200rpm. Riley then claimed that he was satisfied with the aircraft's readiness. At about 8.20pm Riley, with Hamblin in the rear seat, started the engine and taxied across the field. The aircraft trundled over the corn stubble at full power and lifted into the air. It rose to a height of about 100ft and was over some farm buildings when, suddenly, the engine started to mis-fire and it then veered to the right and began to descend. James Riley made every effort to avoid a barn owned by farmer Robert Whitworth but the aircraft nose-dived into the ground. Riley, suffered severe head injuries and was jammed into his seat owing to the front of the engine being crushed in. Corporal Hamblin also suffered head injuries and he was the first to receive attention when rescuers arrived in the form of Mr Blick, of Ford End Road, and two police constables who had been on the riverside patrol at Honey Hills. James Hamblin was conveyed by boat to Kempston Mill, and later to the Bedford County Hospital. The pilot was then removed from the cockpit, but died about five minutes later.

An official report written by the accident investigation team found that the aircraft was in a serviceable condition but that the gap on the spark plugs on No.1 and 3 cylinders were set at less than .002 inches. Subsequently, they felt that the accident occurred as a result of the mechanic failing to set the spark plug gaps correctly and the pilot failing to carry out a proper engine test before taking off. At the request of the farmer the aircraft was removed by Bedfordshire Police and placed at the rear of the Three Tuns public house in Biddenham. At the County Records Office in Bedford you can find an original poster advertising an auction that was held on 11th September 1920 at Honey Hills near Biddenham. It is believed that this poster may refer to the crashed FK8 but describes the aircraft as an Avro No.6. The wreck remained at the Three Tuns until it was eventually auctioned for the princely sum of £6. It is not known if the aircraft ever flew again as no further records are known to exist.

The Site Today

Although the ground behind the Three Tuns has been built upon since the early days of flight it is not hard to envisage the sight of the wrecked FK8 at the rear of the premises and the interest that must have been generated amongst the local population. The site of the crash cannot be precisely located but it is likely to be in the region of the Old Barns, Church End as this is where Robert Whitworth had his farm. In the fields surrounding the area one can only imagine what it must have been like to witness the FK8 falling from the sky as it passed into history to become one of Bedfordshire's first recorded aviation accidents.

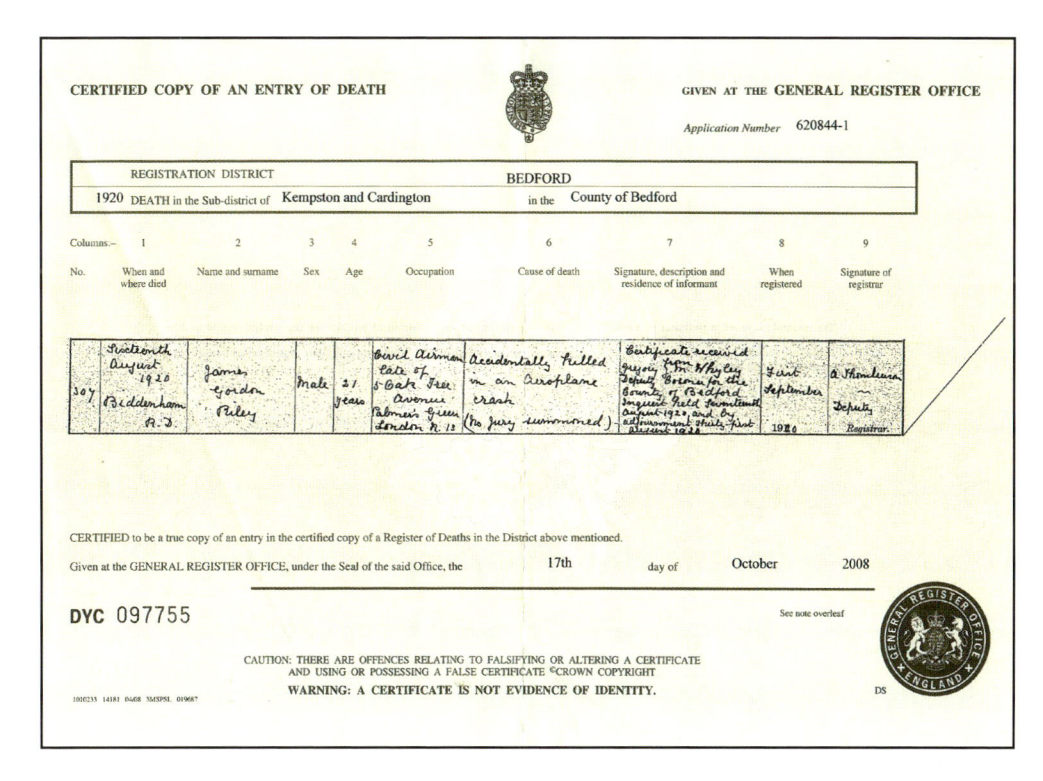

Above: A copy of the death certificate issued for James Riley – one of the first men to die in Bedfordshire as the result of an aircraft accident. (Source: General Records Office)

Below: The Three Tuns public house as it appears today.

MID-AIR COLLISION OVER HENLOW

On Wednesday 10th March 1926 a Vickers Vimy, serial number F9184, of the Inland Area Aircraft Depot was testing parachutes over RAF Henlow. Aboard the massive aircraft were three young aircraftmen who were part of the Parachute Test Unit and at the controls was F/O Charles Lacey. The pilot had a great deal of experience and had obtained his flying certificate at the Royal Naval School in Eastchurch on 23rd May 1913 whilst serving as a naval shipwright. He was commissioned as a lieutenant on 19th May 1915 and was posted to the armed liner Laconia. Lacey then served in the East African campaign where he was stationed at Mombasa, and also aboard HMS Hyacinth, until October 1916 when he was posted to Vendome in

10th March 1926

LOCATION
Henlow

TYPE — **SERIAL No.**
Vickers F.B.27 — F9184

TYPE — **SERIAL No.**
Avro 504K — H5035

UNIT
Inland Area Aircraft Depot

PILOT
Flying Officer William SCOTT
aged 49 - killed

PILOT
Flying Officer Charles Victor LACEY AFC
aged 39 - killed

CREW
Leading Aircraftman Reginald Richard GERMAIN
aged 24 - killed
Leading Aircraftman Basil Henry Groewe YOUNG
aged 23 - killed
Leading Aircraftman James W SIMMONDS
aged 24 - killed

Right: Charles Victor Lacey, the pilot of the Vimy that crashed at Henlow.

Below: The funeral of LAC Basil Young one of the crewmembers.

France. This was a Royal Naval Air Service flight training school and he remained there, probably as an instructor, until 1st August 1919 when he was granted a commission as a Flying Officer in the Royal Air Force. At approximately 11.10am on the day of the crash Lacey was returning to the airfield at Henlow following some parachute trials. As he approached the aerodrome, at a height of about 300 feet, an Avro 504K, Serial Number H5035, piloted by F/O William Scott, appeared out of the clouds and smashed into the underside of the Vimy. The collision sent both aircraft plummeting to earth where they exploded into a fireball, flames reaching a height in excess of 200 feet. The local fire brigade took almost an hour to bring the fire under control, by which time the five airmen aboard had been burnt beyond recognition.

Flying Officer William Scott

William Scott was a Nottingham man. A former postal sorter he had served with the Sherwood Foresters for 20 years and had achieved a commission in the regiment when he arrived in France during WW1. He transferred to the Royal

```
                                                                        489
LACEY, Charles Victor.
     Royal Naval Aviation School, Eastchurch

Born  31st July, 1887,     at   Portsmouth
Nationality  British
Rank or Profession   Shipwright, R.N.
Certificate taken on   Bristol Biplane
At      The Naval School, Eastchurch
Date  23rd May, 1913
```

Left: Chales Victor Lacey's Flying Certificate.

Flying Corps and served in Egypt. In 1918 the RFC became the Royal Air Force and William served for two years in Berlin with the Inter-Allied Commission.

He later moved to RAF Henlow where he was engaged on parachute work. It is believed that he was blinded by the sun as the Avro fighter was climbing and did not see the Vickers Vimy above him. A farm labourer, named Tullady, witnessed the crash. He was working in a field some four miles away and saw the Vickers Vimy dropping parachutes. It was flying very low and circling around, probably in preparation for landing, when he saw the Avro rise up and strike the Vimy. The two aircraft appeared to be locked together as they fell and then a pall of smoke rose up from the ground. Sadly, there were also two more witnesses to the event, the children of Charles Lacey, the Vimy pilot, were at the airfield that day and saw their father's aircraft crash and burn. His wife, who had given birth to another child a few weeks before, was recuperating at home unaware of the tragedy.

Today, the exact location of the crash site is not known but a memorial plaque and brass plate to the pilots and crew can be found in St Andrew's Church, Henlow.

AN ACROBAT DIES OVER CLIFTON

1st July 1928

LOCATION
Clifton Lodge, Henlow

TYPE
Avro 504N

SERIAL No.
H2534

UNIT
23(F) Squadron, Royal Air Force

PILOT
Flight Lieutenant Harold Charles CALVEY, aged 31 - killed

PASSENGER
Flight Sergeant William Charles HOLLIER, aged 35 - killed

The Pilot

Harold Calvey was born in Lewisham on 28th June 1897. The details of his early life are somewhat sketchy but at the outbreak of the First World War, whilst living in Belfast, he applied for a Commission in the Army and, on 17th October 1914, was made a 2nd Lieutenant in the Army Service Corps. Having undergone initial training at The Curragh he was eventually posted to the Supply Unit of the 12th Division as a Supplies Officer. On 29th May 1915 the Division arrived in France for service on the Western Front and after two days of preparation at Boulogne moved to St.Omer in readiness for action in the Flanders area. Harold, however, was left behind in Boulogne to undertake the tedious task of supplying the Division as it took part in some of the decisive actions of the Great War. He never saw action with the Division and remained in the Boulogne/Etaples area for over a year, much to the exasperation of his senior officers. It would appear that Harold, now just 19 years-old, was desperate to take part in the action and counting sandbags was not what he had in mind. Eventually, his seniors opted to recommend that he be discharged from his duties due to 'inefficiency' and he left the Army Service Corps on 11th July 1916. A few weeks later Harold found himself in Oxford where he was to undertake a course of aviation instruction in order that he might enter the Royal Flying Corps.

After completing his training at the Central Flying School, Upavon he was commissioned as a Flying Officer on 4th January 1917. Harold was then posted to No.11 Squadron at Izel-le-Hameau, north of Arras on 14th February 1917. In April of that year, the Allies launched a joint ground offensive, with the

Above: An Avro 504

British attacking near Arras, while the French Nivelle Offensive was launched on the Aisne. Their air forces were called on to provide support, predominantly in reconnaissance and artillery spotting. On 6th April 1917, whilst Harold was taking part in a patrol in the Lens area, his aircraft, an F.E.2b (7695), was hit by anti-aircraft fire, wounding him in his left arm. With his controls damaged he made a crash landing and was knocked unconscious as a result of the impact. He was transferred back to the UK on the hospital ship St.Davis arriving at Dover on 10th April. After a period of recuperation he went on to serve with the Royal Flying Corps on Home Service until it was amalgamated into the Royal Air Force in 1918.

Over the next ten years Harold Calvey became renowned for his aerobatic abilities and attended many air pageants representing the Royal Air Force. On 1st November 1926, flying a specially equipped Sopwith Snipe at Henlow, he established a remarkable record for upside-down flight. From an altitude of about 3,000ft. he circled the aerodrome, upside-down, for a total of 7 minutes and 4 seconds. The following year he is recorded as having given displays of 'Eccentric and Crazy flying' in a Gloster Gamecock whilst serving with No.23 Squadron.

At 6.30pm on 1st July 1928 an Avro 504N, serial number H2534, of 23(F) Squadron was being flown across the evening skies above Henlow by Flight Lieutenant Harold Calvey. In the rear observer's seat was Flight Sergeant William Hollier, the son of a Kent policeman.

The story of what happened that afternoon was recorded in the local newspaper and an extract of their account is as follows;

The fatal aeroplane accident at Clifton on Sunday evening caused deep concern in the village, for the pilot, Flight-Lieutenant Harold Calvey, was very well known there and at Henlow Camp. Before being transferred to Kenley about 18 months ago he was stationed at

Henlow and lived at Clifton Lodge, a residential hotel only a short distance from where he met his death. He had paid frequent visits here since his departure, and would announce his arrival to brother-officers at the hotel by circling three times overhead, sometimes flying upside-down, and doing other 'stunts' before going off to land at Henlow, where his companions would meet him. It is thought that Flight-Lieutenant Calvey was about to follow his usual practice when the accident happened, but as Clifton is on the direct line from London to Sutton Bridge, where he was proceeding for ground firing practice, it may be merely coincidence that the accident occurred at this spot. At all events, the cause of the disaster remains a matter of conjecture. All that is known is that the machine was seen flying at about 1000 feet and approaching the lodge from over the church when without warning it went in to a spiral nose-dive and crashed to the ground. It fell near a corner of Church Close, an open hay field, and the crash was heard several miles away. When the first people from the village reached the spot they found the dead bodies of the pilot and his passenger, Flight-Sergeant W C Hollier, in the middle of the wreckage. The Henlow Aerodrome fire brigade and an ambulance were sent for, and PC Jackson, assisted by members of the RAF and other helpers, extracted the bodies. Mr F Humphreys, the proprietor of Clifton Lodge Hotel, told our representative on Sunday night that he was in the house when at about 6.45, he heard a terrific noise. "I ran out with several officers who were staying at the house" he said, "and saw the smashed aeroplane just across the field."

"At first it was impossible to recognise the occupants, so badly were they injured, and when it was discovered that one of them was Lieut. Calvey we had an awful shock, as he had often stayed with us and was a personal friend." Mrs Humphreys stated that all her husband and two officers were able to do was to send for the ambulance and assist in removing the bodies.

The accident was actually seen by Mr G W Secker, who said that the machine fell at something over a hundred miles an hour with the engine, apparently, running full out until it hit the ground. There was nothing to indicate that anything was wrong until the nose-dive began. Another witness, Mrs Rodwell, who saw the smash from her house about 400 yards away, said that as the machine fell one of the airmen appeared to be waving. She added, "The whole village will mourn for Lieut. Calvey, for everyone here knew him, and there has never been a more popular officer in the village. It is like losing one of our community, and his death happening at a spot that was so familiar to him makes the tragedy seem all the worse." People in the church heard the roar of the Avro's engine during the reading of the Lesson, but no one seems to have attached any undue importance to the noise of the crash that happened a few moments later, and the service proceeded without interruption. However the Rector's wife, Mrs La Porte Payne, who was not at the service, called Mr C Revitt, the lay reader, from the church and informed him of the occurrence and the Rector later announced the sad news to the congregation and offered special prayers on behalf of the bereaved relatives.

Above: The wreckage of Calvey's Avro 504.

Flight-Lieutenant Calvey was about 30 years of age, and leaves a widow and a little boy aged four. On Saturday he took part in the Air Pageant at Hendon, afterwards dining with friends in London. Flight-Sergeant Hollier was also married.

The skill and daring of Flight-Lieut. Calvey as a 'stunt' pilot had won him wide renown in the Air Force, an in the July number of Airways, the air travel magazine, a contributor who writes under the name of 'Observer' says : "On a recent visit to Kenley Aerodrome, I was fortunate enough to arrive just in time to see Flight-Lieutenant Calvey accomplish that extraordinarily difficult aerobatic, the inverted loop. In the manoeuvre, the machine in this case a Hawker 'Hawfinch', is first flown upside down, and then dived to attain sufficient speed for the loop, from which the machine emerges still flying upside down. The feat is not easy of achievement because when upside-down the wings are less efficient and the machine tends to stall more readily than when the right way up. Incidentally, Flight-Lieutenant Calvey, in my opinion, is one of the finest aerobatic pilots in the Royal Air Force."

The Site Today

Today the Clifton Lodge Hotel has disappeared and is known as Clifton Manor. When you pass the site of the crash there is not much to remind you of the events of that summer afternoon so long ago, when visitors could purchase Tea for 1/3d. If you listen carefully you may hear the distant sound of a Lynx engine high in the clouds above or the roar of a crowd as a dare devil pilot demonstrates his death-defying skills. Spare a thought too for Harold Calvey and William Hollier whose lives were cut so tragically short in the skies above Clifton.

FLYING DUCHESS LOSES PRIVATE PILOT AT LIDLINGTON

5th December 1933

LOCATION
Thrupp End Farm, Lidlington

TYPE
GAL ST.4 Monospar

SERIAL No.
G-ACKT

OWNER
Her Grace The Duchess Of Bedford

PILOT
Flight Lieutenant James Bernard ALLEN aged 35 - Killed

Dame Mary Russell, Duchess of Bedford, became interested in aviation late in life and was aged 61 when she took her first flight. She learned to fly so that she could commute more quickly between her estates and also claimed that it provided her with some relief from her constant tinnitus. The 'Flying Duchess', as she became known, undertook several record-breaking flights with her private pilot, Captain Charles Barnard. Before her death in a flying accident in 1937 she owned a number of aircraft. One of these was a state-of-the-art monoplane called a Monospar. Built during the early 1930s by General Aircraft Ltd the Monospar was described as a low wing passenger aircraft. They had an all-metal structure with fabric covering. The first design was the ST-4, a twin-engined monoplane with a fixed tailwheel landing gear. Powered by two Pobjoy R radial engines the first aircraft flew in May 1932 and was followed by five production aircraft.

The ST-4 II, an improved variant with minor differences, followed with a production run of 30. One of these aircraft was ST4/29 with the serial G-ACKT. It was owned by the Duchess of Bedford and on 5th December 1933 was being flown by her private pilot F/Lt James Allen. On that fateful afternoon Ernest Pepper was in the farmyard at Thrupps Farm, Lidlington, when, at about 5.30pm, he saw a bright light in the sky, which was probably the aircraft's forward landing light. A few moments later the aircraft flew in a complete circle at low speed before striking high tension cables and crashing in a field near the farm.

F/Lt Allen was apparently flying back to Woburn from Hooton. According to reports he was flying low, feeling his way in the darkness, perhaps with his engines throttled back a little, and suddenly saw ahead of him, in the light of his head lamp, some high tension cables. To avoid these he did a sudden steep turn, presumably stalled, and dived into the ground. After the crash he was taken to hospital with serious injuries including, a broken thigh, a broken leg, and head injuries but, sadly, died later in the evening.

The Pilot

James Allen was born in Bristol on 23rd February 1897. He had served in the Gloucestershire Regiment from 1914 to 1916 before transferring to the Royal Flying Corps. He was a member of the Royal Air Force when it formed on 1st April 1918 and served with it until 1927. After leaving the service he became the chief instructor and aerodrome manager to the Liverpool and District Aero Club between 1928 and 1930. He was also a member of the Guild of Air Pilots and Navigators and had been one of the Duchess of Bedford's private pilots since 1930.

Above: The Duchess of Bedford pictured in 1933.

The Inquest

At the inquest into the death of F/Lt Allen the following statement was made; "It is strongly suggested that the accident was due to the pilot suddenly finding himself confronted with a pylon of the electricity grid, and losing control of the machine in a sudden turn to avoid it. If that be the case, then the death of a fine pilot must certainly be put down to the debit account of the grid, and, what is more, unless something is done quickly the grid will be the cause of many more deaths. In the last report on Civil Aviation in this country, it was mentioned that the Air Ministry had under consideration three methods of lighting the cables at specially dangerous points. One was by attaching neon tubes to the cables themselves, which was rejected as unsatisfactory.

The second was by indirect lighting from a projector lamp about 25 feet away from the base of the pylon, which was under consideration at the end of the year, and the third was by hanging lamps on lattice masts of the same height as the cables. Naturally, this last scheme was estimated to be very expensive. Now that civil flying is increasing so fast the problem is likely to become very serious, and it is high time that lighting of the pylons should be undertaken with equal seriousness."

A Lesson Learned?

Safety in the aviation industry has moved on in leaps and bounds since the early days of flight. However, some 61 years after the Monospar fell from the Bedfordshire skies, in December 1994, four people died when a light aircraft crashed after hitting an electricity pylon at Stapleford Tawney, in Essex. Firefighters tried to cut the pilot and passengers free from the wreckage but it was too late to save them. The aircraft was approaching an airfield when it hit some power cables and came down in a field. What lessons learned?

Below: The GAL Monospar was quite a futuristic design for its time.

Right: The wreckage of G-ACKT in the field at Thrupp End Farm

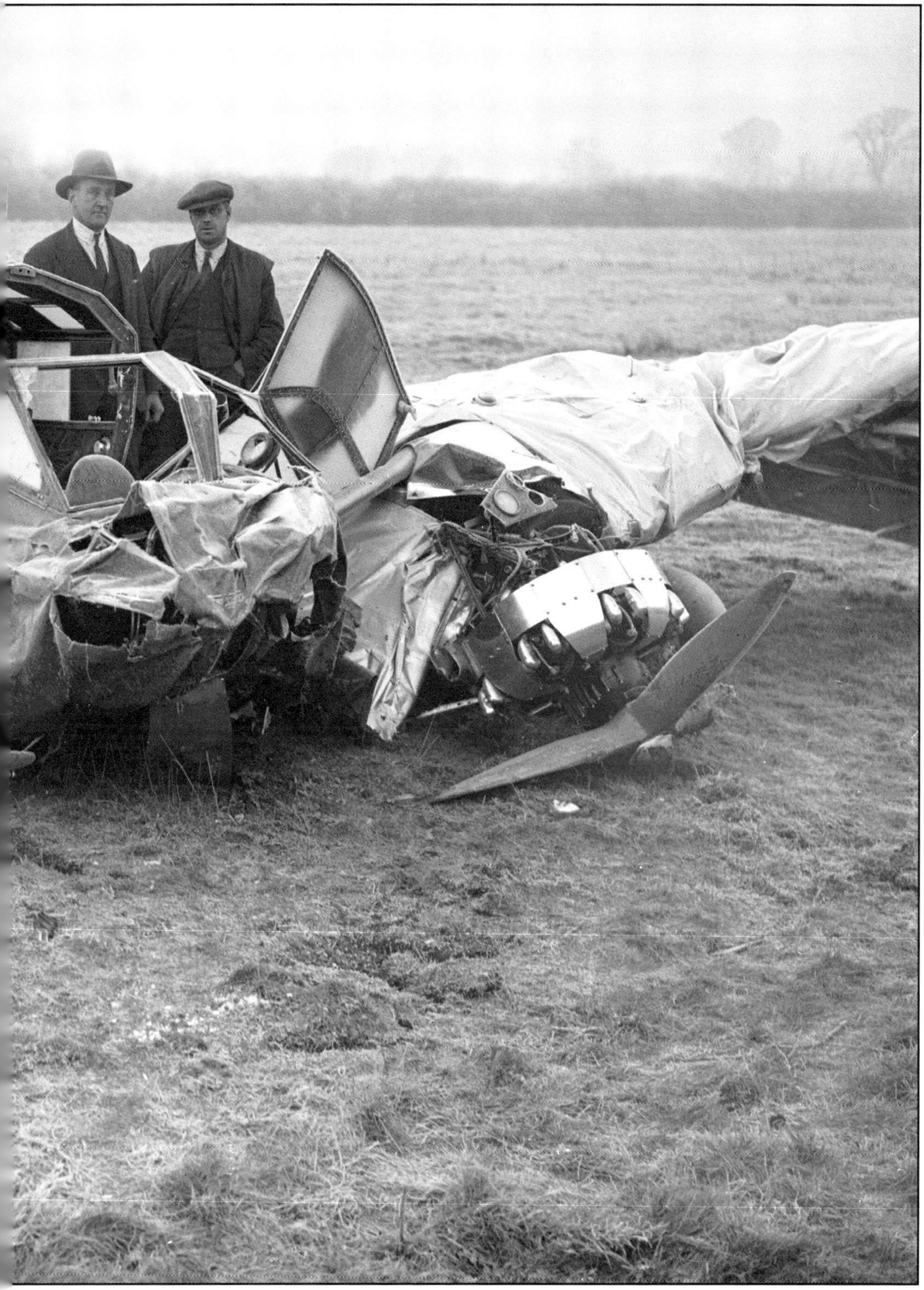

A TIGER ON DUNSTABLE DOWNS

The Pilot

Cuthbert Startup was born in Bishop's Stortford on 18th March 1896, the son of George and Marie Startup. His father was a Wesleyan minister. He Joined the Royal Naval Air Service in November 1914 but his career as a young naval officer was a turbulent one. He spent a great deal of time in hospital with a variation of ailments and at one point was found by his superior officer to be intoxicated. Eventually, the RNAS felt that he was not officer material and on 7th August 1916 his commission was terminated. Records indicate that Cuthbert then went on to join the Royal Artillery and was based at Woolwich Barracks. It was whilst he was stationed in London, in February 1917, that he married Phyllis Preston. In June 1917 Cuthbert transferred to the Royal Flying Corps and achieved a commission as a 2nd Lieutenant on 29th April 1918. He served on the Western Front with both No.88 and No.104 Squadrons. In June 1919 he was involved in a flying accident in which he was seriously burned by an exploding fuel tank. This left him with severe scars to his face, hands and legs. As a result he was invalided out of the service in 1920 but was allowed to retain his rank. Cuthbert spent the next ten years fighting a case for permanent disability until, finally, in 1929 he was granted a 50% disability rating. Sadly, during this period of his life his wife divorced him. He did not take up flying again until 1932 when, on 15th May, he was granted his Glider Pilot's Certificate whilst a member of the London Gliding Club. In the spring of

4th May 1936	
LOCATION	Dunstable
TYPE	de Havilland Tiger Moth
SERIAL No.	G-ADGO
OWNER	The London Flying Club
PILOT	Mr. Cuthbert Lewthwaite STARTUP - seriously injured
PASSENGER	Miss E SMART - fatally injured

1939 Cuthbert married Rosina Mary Crilly and the couple remained together until his death in 1968.

The Accident

At 5.20pm on 24th May 1936, a warm Sunday afternoon, Cuthbert took from Hatfield aerodrome in a de Havilland Tiger Moth (G-ADGO) to undertake a pleasure flight for his passenger, Miss E Smart. After being in the air for about 15 minutes the aircraft was seen flying over the London Gliding Club at Dunstable. Cuthbert put the small aircraft into a dive and zoomed over the clubhouse before flying away. He returned a few minutes later and performed several loops before going into a spin. The aircraft was at a very low altitude when it went into a spin and as Cuthbert brought the aircraft under control he found himself too low to make a full recovery and it struck the ground. Both the pilot and his passenger were seriously injured with Miss Smart eventually succumbing to her injuries. It is not known if Cuthbert ever flew again following this incident but the subsequent investigation found that he was totally responsible for the accident as a consequence of "poor airmanship resulting in the loss of life".

The London Gliding Club

Today the London Gliding Club continues to operate from the clubhouse at Dunstable. Members of the club, which was inaugurated on February 20th 1930, had started gliding by using nearby Ivinghoe Beacon as a launch site but eventually moved to Dunstable Downs. In 1939 Geoffrey Stephenson, a club member, was the first to glide across the Channel when he flew all the way from Dunstable to France. During the Second World War the London Gliding Club was used as a prisoner of war camp and some evidence of this is still visible as a row of posts near the south-west launch point. Since the war the London Gliding Club has steadily grown, but the location of Cuthbert Startup's crash site can no longer be found.

Top: A photo of Startup taken in 1916.

Above: Some 16 years later he posed for this photo to be used on his pilot's licence.

FIRST LOSS AT CRANFIELD

Cranfield officially opened on 1st June 1937, under the control of No.1 Bomber Group. The first RAF aircraft to arrive were the Hawker Hinds of No.108 Squadron from Farnborough. These were soon followed by the Hinds of No.82 Squadron, which had reformed as a light-bomber squadron at RAF Andover on 14th June 1937 and No.62 Squadron which had reformed on 3rd May 1937 at RAF Abingdon. The shadows of war were beginning to form over Europe and activity on the newly formed airfield was heavy. One hazardous practice in which pilots were required to engage was that of taking off and landing at night. On 12th October 1937 the first accident occurred involving the loss of a pilot at night. The Squadron Operations Record Book does not provide any details, but the Bedfordshire Times and Independent reported the incident on 15th October 1937 and their article is outlined below;

12th October 1937	
LOCATION	Cranfield
TYPE	Hawker Hind
UNIT	108 Squadron, Royal Air Force
PILOT	Pilot Officer James Lawrence WELLS aged 21 - killed

"FIRST FATALITY AT NEW AERODROME - Cranfield pilot Killed in Night Landing."

"The first fatal accident at the newly established Cranfield Royal Air Force Station occurred on 12th October at the edge of the aerodrome. An aircraft of No.82 Bomber Squadron which was being flown by Pilot Officer James Lawrence Wells, aged twenty-one, of Edinburgh, struck a tree near the Moulsoe Road and burst into flames. Efforts to save the pilot failed. Pilot Officer Wells, who had been posted to Cranfield for navigation duties after passing a short navigation course, was taking part in night operations. His aeroplane hit one of the trees in a clump attached to Moulsoe Road cottage occupied by Mr Sinfield. It crashed

Above: A Hawker Hind similar to the one that crashed at Cranfield.

to the ground and almost immediately burst into flames. Pilot Officer Wells was the only occupant and he had no chance of escaping. The aerodrome fire squad rushed to the scene, but when the flames had been extinguished the pilot was found to be dead. Squadron Leader N C Pleasance, Officer Commanding No.82 Squadron, said that Wells had been in the Air Force about two years. He last saw him alive at about 6.25pm on Tuesday. Wells had been up and had made one landing. Witness asked him to make another landing, in accordance with the instructions. He went up at once, made a circuit of the Aerodrome, and came round to land in the flare path. He came in at a very low altitude, wide of the flare path, and witness thought it was an error of judgment on his (Wells's) part. He turned to his left, still at low altitude, and hit a tree about fifty feet high. The machine then fell to the ground and caught fire. He and other people rendered all the assistance they could.

The Coroner asked if there was any trouble about the first landing, and the witness replied that there was not. The instructions were to fly forty minutes and make two landings. In reply to another question, [the] witness said that the flare path was to one side of the trees. ... A verdict of accidental death was returned."

THE BATTLE OF CARLTON

Designed in 1933 to replace the Hawker Hart light bomber, the Fairey Battle was to become one of the most notorious aircraft of the Second World War and would suffer devastating losses in the Battle of France. Powered by a single Rolls Royce Merlin engine, it could carry four 250lb bombs in its bomb bay, and two more under the wings. The aircraft carried a crew of three with the pilot and radio operator in a long 'glasshouse' cockpit and the observer in a prone position in the belly of the fuselage. By the summer of 1939 over 2000 had been built and were in service with the RAF.

It was one of these aircraft that, just before mid-day on Friday 11th August 1939, was taking part in a low-level practice raid on the last day of a home defence exercise. The Fairey Battle of 218 Squadron was based at Boscombe Down, Wiltshire and was being flown by a young Australian pilot, F/O William Kinane. He was flying at less than 90ft from the ground when he brought the aircraft swooping over the brow of a hill near Carlton, Bedfordshire. Suddenly, a prominent electricity pylon appeared on the fast moving horizon, but there was nothing Kinane could do about it. The aircraft clipped the top of the structure and the fuel tanks were immediately ignited by the impact. Now trailing flames, it quickly lost height and crashed to the ground 200 yards beyond Northey Farm, near the village of Turvey. The pilot and his observer, Sgt Peter Allan, were killed instantly. The third member of the crew, Aircraftman 1st Class Ivor Roberts, was badly burned and critically injured. He was taken to the Station Sick Quarters at RAF Cranfield where he died two days later.

Today, Sergeant Allen lays buried at Biggin Hill, Kent and Aircraftman Roberts is buried at St. Athan, Wales. Flying Officer Kinane was buried with full military honours on Wednesday 16th August at Cranfield's St Peter and Paul Churchyard, Bedfordshire.

11th August 1939

LOCATION
Northey Farm, Carlton

TYPE
Fairey Battle I

SERIAL No.
K9328

UNIT
218 Squadron, Royal Air Force

PILOT
Flying Officer William KINANE aged 21 - killed

CREW
Sergent Peter ALLAN aged 28 - killed
Aircraftman 1st Class Ivor ROBERTS aged 21 - died of injuries on 13th August 1939

1940

THE GEORGE CROSS IS WON AT CRANFIELD

The Story Of Vivian Hollowday GC MID

Vivian Hollowday was born on 13th October 1916 in Ulceby, Lincolnshire the son of Carl and Annie Hollowday. He joined the RAF in September 1939 with the Service Number 935282 and served with No.14 Service Flying Training School at RAF Cranfield. He was to win the George Cross for exceptional bravery following two separate crashes at Cranfield on the nights of July 2nd 1940 and August 7th 1940, in which he made desperate efforts to rescue the aircrew involved. He had been injured during the first rescue attempt and had only just been released from hospital when the second incident occurred. The official citation for his award can be found in the London Gazette dated 21st January 1941 and reads as follows;

"During August, 1940, this airman was again returning to the camp when an aircraft suddenly spun to the ground and exploded. He immediately went to the crash and a second explosion occurred. Ammunition was exploding all the time but despite this, he borrowed a gas mask, wrapped two sacks over himself and spent some time in the flames, making four attempts before he succeeded in releasing the first occupant. He then re-entered the burning wreckage and successfully removed the second. All three occupants, however, were already dead. Aircraftman Hollowday displayed amazing courage and initiative on both occasions."

After his award, Vivian Hollowday went on to serve with his unit across the UK, and also saw service in Algeria, Sicily and Italy. He was demobilised in 1946 and lived in Bedford where he worked for local grain merchants, Quenby Price. Described as a quiet and unassuming man he was, during his service, apparently reluctant to wear his medal ribbon. His other medals

Above:
Vivian Hollowday
GC MiD.

and awards included the 1939/45 Star, Africa Star, Italy Star, France and Germany Star, Defence Medal, 1939/45 War Medal with MID Oak Leaf, the 1953 Coronation Medal, the Cross for European Confederation, Australian Bronze Medal, Cross of French Societe des Anciens Combattants, and the Belgian Albert I Merit Cross with One Gold and One Silver Palm. In 1971, whilst staying in a London hotel, his medals were stolen and a duplicate set had to be produced. Sadly, Vivian died on 15th April 1977, aged 61, and he was cremated in Bedford where his ashes were interred. In 1986, his widow offered his medals for auction at Sotheby's and they were purchased by the Royal Air Force Museum, where they can now be found on display. There appears to be some uncertainty around the events that led to the award being made and my research, based on accident reports located in the National Archives in Kew, have led me to believe that the following incidents were those that involved Vivian Hollowday.

On the night of 2nd July 1940 Sgt Noel Davies had been given 55 minutes' dual tuition with his instructor Flight Sergeant Darling, which was completed at 23.20 hrs. It was then decided that Sgt Davies, who had previously flown a Harvard aircraft solo, should undertake a number of take-off and landings in a solo aircraft and was switched to Master N7695, which had been fitted with additional ballast weights. The weather was now calm, with no low cloud and a definite horizon, as Sgt Davies opened the throttle of the small aircraft and made a normal take off. Flight Sergeant Darling stated that he had watched the aircraft make a series of climbs and turns and fly parallel with the airfield's flare path, after which it disappeared behind some trees. It then re-appeared and was seen making a steep climb when it suddenly turned and dived into the ground on the airfield boundary. At this point AC1 Vivian Hollowday, who was off duty and on his way back to camp, witnessed the aircraft crash and burst into flames. He immediately ran to the wreckage and made his way through the burning debris, which was scattered over a wide area by the force of the impact. He found the pilot, whose clothing was on fire, and put the flames out with his bare hands. Sadly, Sergeant Davies was already dead

2nd July 1940

LOCATION
Cranfield

TYPE
Miles Master

SERIAL No.
N7695

UNIT
14 Service Flying Training School

PILOT
Sergeant Noel Francis Lloyd DAVIES aged 20 - killed

but had he not been killed instantly in the crash the actions of Vivian Holloway would, in all probability, have saved his life.

The Investigation

Accident Investigators felt that the pilot may have been using visual aids, rather than his instruments, to establish his position, which was an instruction given to him by Flight Sergeant Darling. They believed that this was a contributory factor towards the cause of the accident and recommended that, in future, trainee pilots should be instructed to use instruments when night flying rather than visual aids. It was also felt that it may have been better if Sgt Davies had continued to use the same aircraft in which he had been flying earlier, rather than switching to an alternate. The recommended changes to these two practices would have a significant impact for future trainees and may well have saved many more needlessly lost lives.

7th August 1940

LOCATION
Rincroft Field, Mertlands Farm, North Crawley, Buckinghamshire

TYPE
Bristol Blenheim IV

SERIAL No.
P4902

UNIT
17 Operational Training Unit, Royal Air Force

PILOT
Flight Lieutenant Edward Patrick MORTIMER aged 29 - killed

CREW
Sergeant David Alan GIBBS aged 20 - Observer - killed
Sergeant Frank ALVES aged 21 - Air Gunner - killed

On the night of 7th August 1940 Flight Lieutenant Mortimer and his crew were taking part in a night-flying training exercise and were instructed to fly a route from RAF Upwood to Bicester, a distance of 53 miles. Here he was to alter course and fly to Northampton, a further 25 miles, and, from there return to base which was another 33 miles. The Blenheim made a normal take off from Upwood and flew to Bicester, after which it was seen about 20 miles off course close to RAF Cranfield, where night-flying practice was also taking place. When the aircraft was opposite the Wireless Telegraphy Station it was seen to stagger and then, a few seconds later, lost speed and spun into the ground from a height of about 1500 feet.

An accident investigation later determined that the aircraft had struck the ground at a moderate speed after flattening out from a left-handed spin and had caught fire immediately after the crash. The report further states that; "one body was found in the navigator's compartment and one in the gunner's cockpit. The third, that of the pilot, was lying face down 72 yards east of the wreckage and he had evidently fallen from a considerable height. His parachute was unopened and was on the ground 4 feet away. The rip-cord had not been pulled and examination of the pilot's parachute harness showed that the release ring had not been turned and while in the locked position had been driven back by direct impact on the front. This had forced the spring-loaded plunger out through the aluminium casing and had released the catches and then the harness. From this it may be seen that the harness was in position on the pilot's striking the ground". There was some consternation as to how he had become separated from his parachute. The investigators determined that the pilot had been attempting to locate RAF Cranfield and, after losing sight of the airfield's flare path, had suddenly become aware of the risk of collision with other aircraft from Cranfield. As a result, he had stalled the aircraft which then led to the crash. There is no reference made in the report to the actions of Aircraftman Hollowday. The bodies of F/Lt Mortimer and Sgt Alves are buried in the Bury Cemetery, Cambridgeshire and Sgt Gibbs is buried in his home town of Paignton, Devon.

Above: Flt Lt Edward Mortimer, the pilot of the Blenheim that crashed at Mertlands Farm.

This appears to be the second aircraft referred to in Vivian Hollowday's citation, however, there are some discrepancies. The citation states that he rescued the first occupant, probably the pilot, and that he then returned to the wreckage and removed a second occupant. The accident investigator's report confirms that the pilot was found some distance from the crash site, which may have been as a result of Hollowday's actions. It then states that the other two crew members were found in their positions, which is contradictory to the citation. It must be appreciated that, at the time of writing their report, the investigators must have been under enormous pressure to establish the cause of the accident given the high level of crashes, both through training and combat, that were happening all over the country. It still, however, seems strange that the heroic actions made by Vivian Hollowday had not been taken into account by the investigators when making their report.

FIERY COMET FALLS FROM THE DARK SKIES

by Julian Evan Hart

6th October 1940

LOCATION
Netherstead, near Colmworth

TYPE
Junkers 88 A-5

SERIAL No.
8045

UNIT
4/KG30

PILOT
Oberfeldwebel Gerhard WILKENING aged 27 - killed

CREW
Feldwebel Georg KOSHCHELLA aged 24 - killed
Unteroffizier Heinz THAL aged 28 - killed
Unteroffizier Alexander BEDNAREK aged 23 - killed

A few hours earlier 4D+HM had taken off from Holland and headed out over the North Sea to England. The cause of the crash was never established, although some sources state that it had been subjected to a night fighter attack, others that it was a victim of AA fire. Wartime reports and subsequent excavations revealed no evidence for either. During one dark evening in October 1940 the residents of the small village of Colmworth began to hear the sound of an aeroplane, which was nothing unusual, but this one was clearly in trouble. The shriek and whine of aero engines under full power got louder, and those who looked up into the night sky spotted something like a fiery comet plummeting earthwards with showers of sparks and flames belching from it. One of those who woke up, flung the sheets aside to run over to his window to look up into the night sky was seven year-old John Hughes who recalled "flames streaking from the aeroplane as it fell". The whole countryside seemed to reverberate with this awful noise until there was a loud crash and explosion somewhere near the old Netherstead Farm on the eastern edge of Colmworth. The impact was so violent that the engines and undercarriage assemblies punched down almost twenty feet into the soil. The resulting explosion both forced wreckage deeper as well as scattering compressed wreckage all over the area.

Left: The smoking hole left by the Junkers Ju88 that crashed at Netherstead.

Opposite page: Metal propeller blades usually survive even the most fierce explosions, as is the case with this one retrieved from the Netherstead crash site.

Upon impact at least one propeller blade sheared away. Contorted and torn with the force, it lay nearby. Now all was silent. The next morning the crater and debris from the Junkers were clearly visible from Honeydon Road. Locals now began to learn that the previous evening's comet fireball some of them had witnessed was indeed the demise of a German bomber. The crash site was roped off and a couple of RAF personnel were placed on guard. Smoke still emanated from partially buried sections of the aeroplane and the air was heavy with the smell of hot metal, burned rubber and human flesh. Many small fragments of twisted airframe lay outside the cordoned-off area. Local lad John Hughes actually cycled down to the crash site the following morning. Although he could not get near to the impact point he did see something quite shocking to a seven year old boy; there laying on the grass was a human hand still partially wearing its flying glove.

John said, "It was burned and the smell from it was awful; I can still smell it today." It was said that many other parts and tatters of uniform from the Junkers' crew were tangled up in the branches of nearby trees, John also confirmed this to me some 69 years later when I spoke to him on the telephone in 2009. The crater was so large that it was assumed that bombs had probably been carried deep into the ground upon impact and exploded. One Luftwaffe *ausweis* for Heinz Thal was recovered having been issued at Perleberg on the 13th March 1940. In addition to this a ration card was also found bearing the markings '4/K.G 1940 September'.

The local 'Circular' Newspaper carried the following report:-

GERMAN RAIDER'S CRASH. BLOWN TO PIECES BY ITS OWN BOMBS. COUNTRYSIDE LIT UP BY FIRE. An enemy bomber, believed to be of the Junkers type, crashed in the middle of a grass field, a few miles from a Midland town, early on Sunday morning. Apparently it was still carrying bombs, for there was a terrific explosion. The machine literally disintegrated into small pieces, some of which were thrown two hundred yards and landed in adjoining fields. The machine's crew of three or four men was blown to pieces, and nothing was found by which they might be identified, except some fragments of uniform. Where the bomber crashed was a crater, and from this hole flames were still coming on Sunday afternoon. It was thought that petrol was burning below ground. There were occasional reports as ammunition exploded deep down in the inferno. There was no damage to local property or injury to local persons, but the charred body of a hen pheasant was found near to the crater, a few inches away from the twisted remains of the plane's machine gun. Parts of ammunition belts were strewn about, but beyond these scarcely anything was recognisable. Pieces of engine cowling were found 200 yards away.

WARDEN`S STORY. Buildings a mile away were shaken by the explosion. Flames were plainly visible for a distance of seven miles. A local air raid warden told the following graphic story. "It was a terrible night, much wind and rain, and I was on duty. The peculiar roar of the German engine attracted my attention and I looked up to see an object which resembled a meteorite streaking across the sky and getting gradually lower. Then it seemed to go into a dive about half a mile away, and there was a final roar from the engines before it hit the ground. The explosion seemed to rock the whole district and everything was lighted up in a fierce red glow as I scrambled through hedges, and stumbled over plough land in the direction of the wreck. Finally I reached an opening in the hedge round the meadow in which the plane fell, but the heat was so intense I could go no further. In any case I knew that nothing could be alive after the explosion and outbreak of fire.

A SHATTERING EXPLOSION. Captain M.A.Mackintosh a local farmer described the fall of the bomber as a, "rising scream getting louder and louder and ending in a shattering explosion. We thought it was coming down on top of our house" he said. A Londoner who had come into the country to get some

Below: The Junkers Ju88 was regarded as the best of all the German bombers that took part in the Battle of Britain.

relief from continual bombing said, "I am used to the sound of dive bombers, and when I heard the high pitched roar of the engines, I thought it was Jerry trying to dive bomb something in the locality.

The machine seemed to be directly overhead and I was feeling a bit scared when the roar of the engines ended in a loud explosion about three-quarters of a mile away. Many sightseers and souvenir hunters tried to reach the spot when daylight came, but the field was quickly put 'out of bounds' and only people with official or special missions were allowed to approach the crater.

An excavation by the London Air Museum in the 1970s recovered both Junkers Jumo engines, undercarriage legs, tyres, eight oxygen bottles, one parachute and a first aid kit, complete with safety pins and a bone saw. It was re-excavated in 1986 and many other interesting items were recovered including manufacturer's labels and a parachute 'D'Ring. Other personal items recovered included a tattered leather wallet containing some Dutch coinage. Some parts of this aircraft are currently displayed at Station X Bletchley Park. In 2008 pieces of the Junkers 88 in the form of mangled MG15 bullet casings, Plexiglas sections and gold coloured anodised metal fragments were still clearly discernible amongst the plough soil, small crumpled and twisted reminders of a far off time when the violence of war could unexpectedly and quite literally drop in on you.

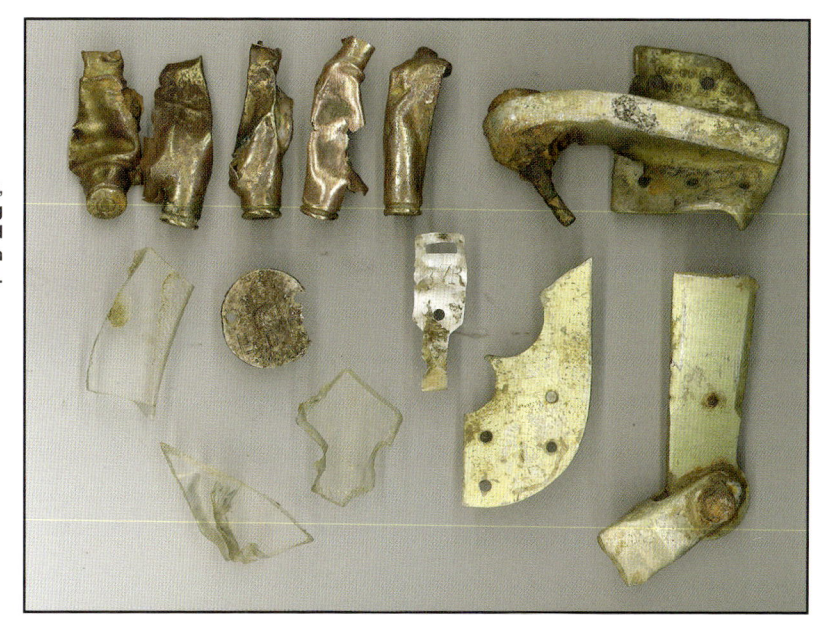

Right: To this day, fragments are still being found in the ploughed soil, like this selection recovered in 2008.

LOCAL LAD FLIES INTO A TREE AT TURVEY

James Bridge was born on 28th May 1914 at 12 Egerton Road, Bexhill, Sussex, the son of Walter and Mary Bridge. His family later moved to Pavenham and, between 1923 and 1933, Jim attended both Bedford Preparatory School and Bedford Modern School. He then went on to attend Bedford Technical Institute and it was here, in October 1934, that Jim, with the support of his employer, W. H. Allen Sons & Co. of Queens' Engineering Works, Bedford, embarked on a mechanical engineering course. On 1st October 1935, Jim enlisted in the Royal Air Force Reserve which had been set up to train volunteer pilots for the service. On 26th June 1939 Jim married Masie Edwina Frazer-Barnes, a 24 year-old secretary, at All Saints, Luton and, after a brief honeymoon spent at the Rose and Crown in Tring, the couple moved into 136 Hurst Grove, Bedford. A few weeks later, on 2nd September, Jim was recalled from the reserve and commenced his war service. He served at No. 9 Flying Training School based at RAF Hullavington, and No. 10 Bombing and Gunnery School at Warmwell, Dorset. After this, Jim went on to Central Flying School in Upavon, Wiltshire where he undertook a Flying Instructor's Course. On 20th May 1940, as the Germans raced across France and an invasion of Britain looked like a distinct possibility, Jim and Maisie saw the arrival of a son, Noel James. On 4th June 1940, a few days after the birth of his son, Jim arrived at RAF Cranfield to take up his duties as a Flying Instructor with No.14 Service Flying Training School. The Battle of Britain raged on in the skies above the

7th October 1940

LOCATION
Newton Park Farm, Turvey

TYPE
Airspeed Oxford I

SERIAL No.
N4729

UNIT
14 Service Flying Training School, Royal Air Force

PILOT
Flying Officer James Frederick BRIDGE (Instructor) aged 26 - killed

CREW
Leading Aircraftman Jack Henry KISSNER aged 23 - Pilot Under Training - killed

Home Counties and instructors were told to keep training flights to a level where they would not interfere with operations.

At 3.30pm on the afternoon of 7th October 1940, Jim Bridge took to the air in an Airspeed Oxford, N4729. His pupil was Leading Aircraftman Jack Kissner, a local lad from nearby Northampton. Their task was to carry out a low flying practice flight around Cranfield. A few moments after leaving the ground the small twin-engined aircraft struck a tree near the end of the runway and crashed between the road and former railway line near Newton Park Farm, one mile south-south-west of the village of Turvey. The aircraft burst into flames on impact with the ground and the two crewmen died instantly.

A subsequent Court of Inquiry found that pilot was flying less than 100 feet above the ground and had flown into bright sun, which hampered his vision. It was also stated that, although Jim had a total of nearly 500 flying hours, he had not had much experience of flying dual in an Oxford and this may have been a contributory factor. Jim Bridge is buried in Bedford Cemetery and Jack Kissner is buried in the St.Peter & St.Paul Churchyard, Cranfield, Bedfordshire.

Above right: Flying Officer James Bridge with his wife and new born son.

Below: An Airspeed Oxford, the type in which he was killed on 7th October 1940.

RARE RECONAISSANCE TYPE AT EATON SOCON

by Julian Evan Hart

This aircraft was engaged on a photo-reconnaissance mission to Coventry and Birmingham when it was spotted and attacked by Hurricanes of No. 1 Squadron. Flight Lieutenant M.H Brown, Pilot Officer A.V. Clowes and Pilot Officer A. Kershaw repeatedly attacked the Dornier literally peppering it with bullet strikes. Each fighter jinked from side to side behind the bomber to get in a burst of fire. 0.303 bullets strikes spattered into the tail section flaking off the paintwork in large areas around each strike. Elongated and jagged edged holes and tears were created by each impact as well as dents and gouges. More bullets struck along the fuselage and into the cockpit, injuring the crew. There was no way this enemy aeroplane was going to return to base, subjected to such a withering hail of bullets. As the combat passed over the village of Bolnhurst small pieces of burning debris from the Dornier set fire to the roof of a thatched cottage. The enemy aircraft with both engines smoking began a shallow dive before it exploded at low altitude scattering large sections over 120 metres across fields at Little End. The three dead airmen's bodies were collected from the site and for a short period were placed in a local barn. One local lad crept into the poorly lit barn determined to have a look at a Jerry airman. Just as he lifted the corner of a blanket, someone came in and

24th October 1940

LOCATION
Fields beside the Crown Inn at Eaton Socon

TYPE
Dornier Do 215B

SERIAL No.
0060

UNIT
3/Aufklarungs. Gruppe Ober der Luftwaffe (Aufkl.Gr.Ob.d.L.)

PILOT
Leutnant E. MAYER - baled out too low and killed

CREW
Gefreiter M. DORR - baled out and captured badly injured
Unteroffizier E. HOFFMANN - baled out too low and killed
Unteroffizier H. BROENING - baled out too low and killed

Above: One of the pilots involved in the shooting down of the Eaton Socon Dornier was Pilot Officer 'Taffy' Clowes seen here with his Hurricane decorated with his famous wasp nose-art.

told him to get out of there. Many years later this eye-witness would recall that one of the things he could clearly remember was that the blanket 'felt very sticky'. Another eye-witness to this event was seven year old John Hughes who lived at nearby Colmworth, he already had some experience of encountering the Luftwaffe when he witnessed the Junkers 88 crash there just some eighteen days previously. Some sixty-nine years later John would recount to the author "I remember hearing all this noise some miles off and looking outside I saw all the aeroplanes wheeling about behind a solitary one.

"I could hear gunfire and suddenly the aeroplane in front caught fire and went down out of sight."

The St Neots Advertiser reported that -

The many people who were in the streets of St. Neots on Thursday (Market Day) had the gratification of seeing a German plane shot down by English planes. The first notification was a burst of gun-fire, and then the planes were seen fighting over Eaton Socon. The enemy plane almost immediately lost height, smoke poured from it, and it fell into a field at Little End, Eaton Socon...On reaching the ground, the plane burst into flames and was soon a wreck. The crew of four all baled out. Three were picked up dead, and the fourth was badly wounded and taken to hospital. All four had been hit by bullets. An eye-witness describes the fight as a 'very clever piece of work.'

(St Neots Advertiser 25th October 1940)

The following week further reports added -

Mr. Albert Mardlin, who was driving a tractor when the wounded airman landed in the field, told a newspaper reporter: "I rushed up to him to see if he was armed. I discovered that he had no weapons of any sort and as I searched him he held his hands in the air and smiled. In one of his pockets he had some cigarettes, so I took one out and gave it to him. The occupants of a farmhouse about a mile away from the scene of the crash were surprised when a door of the plane fell near their house."

(St Neots Advertiser 1st November 1940)

Above: The Dornier 215 was very similar in appearance to the Dornier 17, the main difference being the inline engines on the 215 as opposed to radials on the 17.

The death and tragedy that spread itself across the fields behind the Crown Inn was not restricted to this Thursday. The very next day a young 16 year old RAF engine fitter Harry Clack and 2nd Class Aircraftman Harold Frank Hooker would also die here whilst a third man Leading Aircraftman James Leatherland would be burned. Harry Clack born in Croydon was just 16 when he was assisting in the recovery of the Dornier's wreckage. Harry and the two other men were assisting in the salvage of one of the Dornier's engines with a recovery crane when the jib touched some over head power lines carrying 11,000 volts, and they were all electrocuted. Harry William Clack had only just completed his accelerated training on October 5th 1940, and was then posted to Cambridge on salvage and repair duties. His tragic death on 25th October 1940 means that Harry Clack was the youngest member of the RAF to die in World War Two as a result of enemy action. He was later buried in plot 6363 in Cambridge City Cemetery. The inquest into this tragic accident was actually held at the Crown Inn just a few yards from where the Dornier fell and a total of five men had been killed.

Excerpts of Coroner's Inquest statements

Corporal Arthur Frank Baker said that on Friday, October 25th, he was in charge of a breakdown gang of eight men. They proceeded to Eaton Socon to pick up a wrecked aircraft. The crane had been taken into the field and was on the job. He went down to see what conveyance was wanted. He looked round and saw three airmen lying on the ground near the crane. He did not see them fall. He shouted for the police and ambulance. A high tension cable ran across the ground, he did not see it until after the accident. The crane had passed beyond the cable when he saw it. He would not have thought the jib of the crane would have come in contact with the cable because of the height of the cable. Aircraftman George Harris deposed.

He drove an RAF crane into a field at Eaton Socon and picked up a damaged aeroplane engine. He had got the engine on the jib and was driving out into the next field when he saw three men running. He stopped as he thought the engine had become unhooked. Instead, he saw three men lying on the ground. On looking up he saw overhead a high tension cable. P.C. Ernest Jakes, Keysoe, said that with P.C. Marlow he was on duty on the Great North Road, Eaton Socon, controlling traffic. He saw the breakdown crane and low lorry arrive to collect the wreckage of the aeroplane. He saw the crane driven into the field and go to the wreckage. There was some difficulty in getting into the field. Later, he heard a shout, went into the field and saw an overhead electric cable swaying about, the jib of the crane was about 3 ft. off the cable. Three men were lying on the ground, all were groaning. One recovered and was taken to hospital. Artificial respiration was tried on the other two men for an hour without avail. The cable poles were 33 ft. high, they carried three wires. From the lowest wire there would be a clearance of 30 ft., but this low wire sagged a bit in the

Below: The charred rear fuselage of the Dornier at Eaton Socon.

Above: The perfect souvenir, the port tail fin of the Dornier complete with swastika and bullet strikes!

middle. There was a mound of earth, about a foot high, underneath the cables, this would be sufficient to raise the crane to come in contact with the cable. As the crane was standing when he went up the top looked almost level with the wire. The cable was not damaged. The cable carried 11,000 volts. There was a big danger notice at the entrance to the field. The coroner could not understand why the driver did not see this, whereby after listening to eye-witness accounts the coroner, Mr R.G. Rose, decided upon a verdict of 'Accidental Death' in each case. According to the St Neots Advertiser as below, the pilot who dealt the Dornier its final blow would himself be killed shortly afterwards.

"Another tragic sequel was the death of the pilot who had dealt the finishing blow to the Dornier that had crashed in Eaton Socon. While engaged in air operations Sergeant.-pilot Robert Dudley Hogg, of 59, The Grove, Bedford, son of Mrs. Hogg and the late Dr. E.H. Hogg had been killed. The young pilot had been flying three months and the Dornier was the second bomber he had destroyed."

(St Neots Advertiser Friday November 22nd, 1940)

However research by the author can only come up with the fact that Robert Dudley Hogg died on 11th November 1940 aged 22 whilst with No 17 Squadron RAFVR. Only the names of the three RAF pilots at the beginning of this section can be established as to being directly involved in this Dornier's demise.

The Crash Site Today

Many years ago the author searched the crash site area to the west of the A1 motorway which was built after the crash and now bisects the crash site. Several small fragments of alloy were spotted in the plough soil and two RAF issue brass spoons have been found at the crash site….probably from the crash recovery crew. Several fragments of airframe still bore traces of white green and black paint. Aviation archaeologist Peter Stanley searched the site and found the metal back-plate of a wristwatch and several fired 0.303 bullets from where the Dornier's tail section had lain. However the sections of crash site to the east of the A1 have now been developed in the last decade and extensively built upon.

Below: Military personnel and policemen survey the scattered remains of the Dornier at Eaton Socon.

1941

BALE OUT OVER HUSBORNE CRAWLEY

On 9th September 1941 a Handley-Page Hampden of No.50 Squadron, piloted by Sergeant Ford Rowney, was returning from a raid on Kassel, Germany, when it became lost. The Hampden, a twin-engine medium bomber serving with the Royal Air Force during the Second World War, bore the brunt of the early bombing war over Europe, taking part in the first night raid on Berlin and the first 1,000-plane raid on Cologne. The newest of the three medium bombers, the Hampden, known as the 'Flying Suitcase' because of its cramped crew conditions, was unsuited to the modern air war.

Eventually, the aircraft began to run short of fuel and two of the crew, Sgt Mitchell and Sgt Morgan, were ordered to bale out, which they did successfully. A local girl, Betty Stapleton, living in Crow Lane described how, in the middle of the night, the sound of the plane could be heard as it passed over the village and came in low. A couple of the crew managed to bale out, but one airman got his parachute caught up in the top of one of the high elm trees that used to line the road, and was left dangling upside down from its branches. The young airman began calling out for help and his cries were heard right across the fields. Her father, Bert, ran to his aid and climbed right to the top of the tree to release him.

9th September 1941

LOCATION
Husborne Crawley

TYPE
Handley-Page Hampden I

SERIAL No.
AD854   VN - ?

UNIT
50 Squadron, Royal Air Force

PILOT
Sergeant Ford ROWNEY
aged 23 - killed

CREW
Flight Sergeant Thomas Anthony BARKER - killed
Sergeant MORGAN - baled out
Sergeant MITCHELL - baled out

Right:
Flight Sgt Thomas Anthony Barker.

Far right:
Sgt Ford Rowney.

Below: An AD serialled 50 Squadron Hampden, identical to the one that crashed at Husborne Crawley.

The aircraft continued to circle the area in the darkness, the pilot apparently searching for a friendly airfield or safe landing place. Then, starved of precious fuel, its engines cut out and the plane came down in a field in Horsepool Lane, on the outskirts of Husborne Crawley, taking the lives of the pilot and wireless operator with it. Flight Sergeant Barker is buried in the Mansfield Cemetery, Nottinghamshire and Sergeant Rowney is buried in St.Wilfreds Churchyard, Arley, Warwickshire.

DEATH OF A BEDFORD SCHOOLBOY

The Squadron

No.601 Squadron was formed at RAF Northolt on 14th October 1925 as a light bomber unit of the Auxiliary Air Force.

The idea for part-time reserve squadrons had been introduced by Lord Trenchard, Chief of the Air Staff, in the early 1920s and, quite simply, was a plan to recruit and use keen amateur pilots in time of war, but keep them in the reserve in times of peace. It was a cheaper option to having more squadrons of full-time fliers and by the time World War Two broke out there were fourteen auxiliary squadrons in the RAF, making up a quarter of Fighter Command.

No.601 was to become known as the *Millionaires' Squadron*, a name gained because of a reputation for filling its ranks with wealthy aristocratic young men. Most of these affluent young pilots had little regard for the rigid discipline of the regular service. They lined their uniform tunics with bright red silk, wore blue ties rather than the regulation black and most of the pilots owned their own private aircraft. In January 1927 the squadron moved to Hendon, which was to remain its base up to the outbreak of the war. On 1st July 1934 the squadron was re-designated a fighter unit flying Hawker Harts, which it retained until August 1937. Just days before the German invasion of Poland in 1939, No.601 Squadron, now flying Blenheims, was mobilised. By March 1940 the squadron had converted to Hurricanes and, during the German invasion of France, a detachment operated from French soil for a week. In July 1940 the squadron was stationed at RAF Tangmere in West Sussex, and participated heavily in

---

19th October 1941

LOCATION
Greyfriars Walk, Bedford

TYPE
Bell P-39 Airacobra I

SERIAL No.
AH582 UF-N

UNIT
601 Squadron, Royal Air Force

PILOT
Pilot Officer Peter Norman HEWITT aged 19 - killed

Opposite page top: 601 Squadron Airacobras all lined up for a press day to introduce the new fighter to the public on 17th October 1941.

Opposite Page bottom: Two days later and the third aircraft in line AH582, UF-N crashed into a house in Bedford, killing its 19 year old pilot.

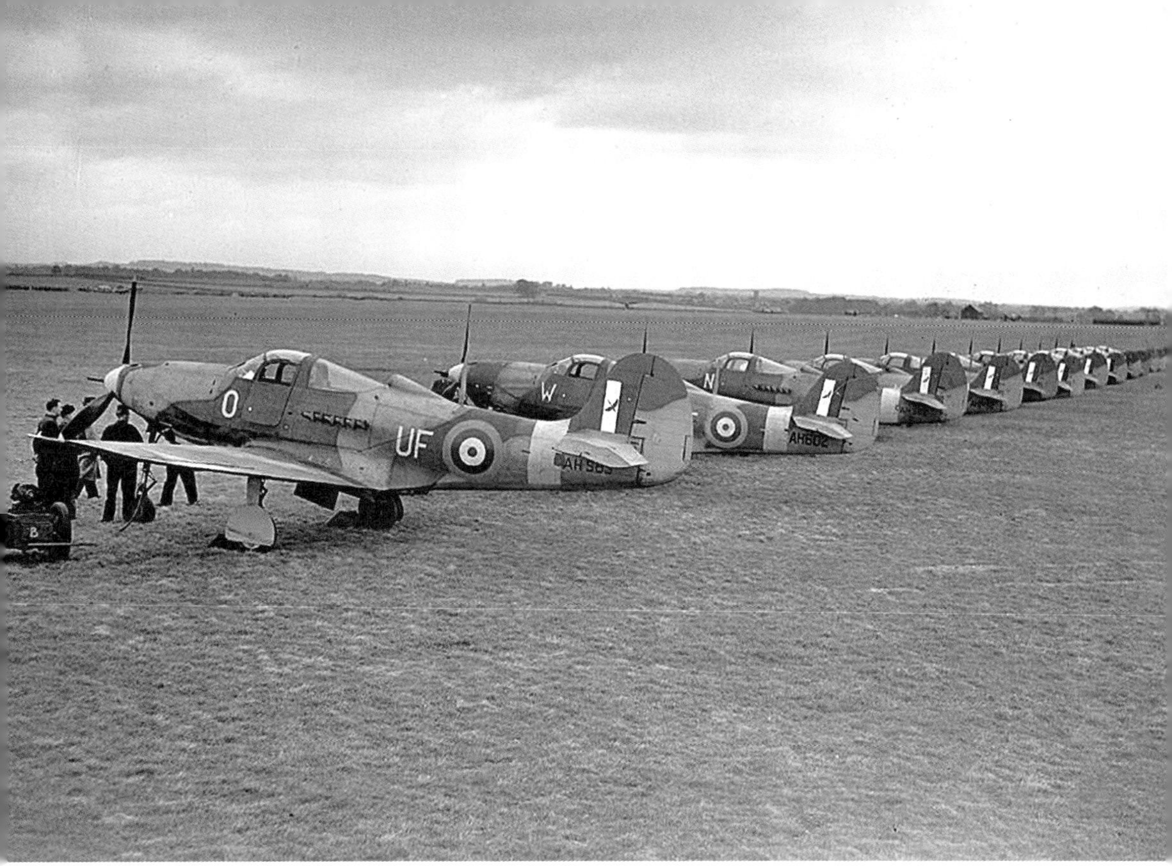
O
UF
W
N
AH602

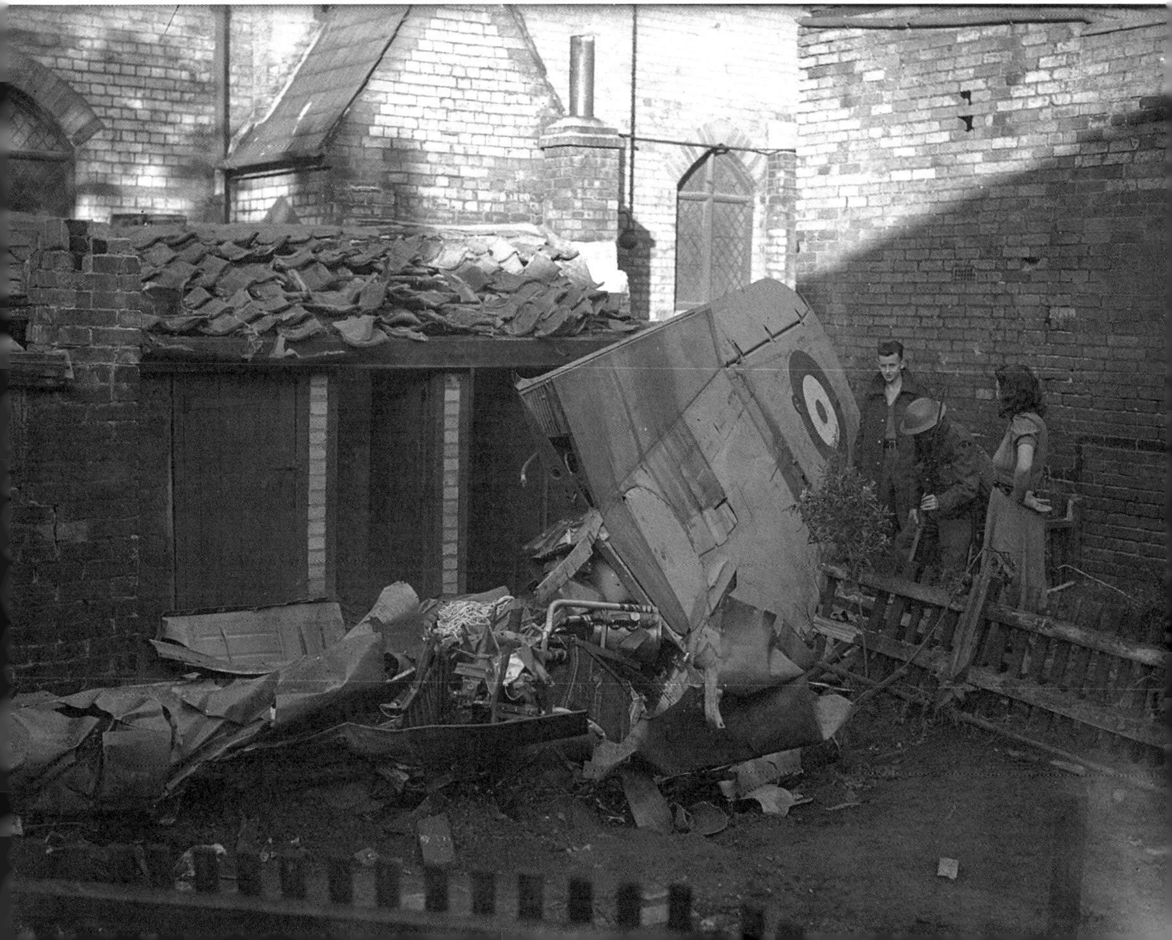

the Battle of Britain. The sustained combat quickly took its toll on the pre-war personnel and, as replacements were drafted in from all walks of life and all parts of the Commonwealth, the squadron became as cosmopolitan as any other. In August 1941 the squadron arrived at RAF Duxford in Cambridgeshire and was re-equipped with American Bell Airacobras. The employment of this aircraft was to prove disastrous for the unit and the RAF and after numerous accidents, some of which were fatal, they were recognised as having an inadequate rate of climb and performance at altitude for Western European conditions. Only 80 were ever adopted, all of them with 601 Squadron. They were discarded in March 1942 in favour of Spitfires.

The Pilot

Peter Hewitt was a great contender for the *Millionaires' Squadron*, being the son of Flight Lieutenant Edward Norman and Mrs Cecilia Ruth Hewitt and the grandson of Sir Tom Percy Woodhouse, who had gained the rank of Major-General in the service of the Army Medical Service. Peter had attended the prestigious Bedford School between 1934 and 1940. The school had a prominent military connection and four of its old boys were to win Victoria Crosses.

It had also produced a number of notable members of the Royal Air Force including Sir Charles Burnett, Sir Thomas Pike and Brian Kingcome. It was only natural that Peter, once he had completed his education, should then follow his father into the service of the Royal Air Force.

The Accident

In February 1941 the squadron had begun taking part in offensive sweeps over northern France, which it continued to do until August, when it began re-equipping with Airacobras. On 19th October 1941 P/O Peter Hewitt took off from RAF Duxford at 13.40 hours to carry out flying practice in clouds. Twenty minutes after leaving the ground the aircraft was seen carrying out aerobatic manoeuvres over Bedford. It would appear that Peter was giving his old school chums a demonstration of his flying abilities, but the aircraft went into a steep uncontrollable dive and crashed into the back garden of a house in Greyfriars Walk, Bedford. A court of enquiry later determined that the accident was due to loss of control whilst the pilot was carrying out aerobatics below a height of 5,000 feet, which was contrary to flying orders. Peter Hewitt's name is recorded on Panel 2, Golders Green Crematorium, London.

CHRISTMAS EVE CRASH IN KEMPSTON

24th December 1941

LOCATION
West End Farm, Kempston

TYPE
Short Stirling I

SERIAL No.
N6066

UNIT
26 Conversion Flight, Royal Air Force

PILOT
Sergeant Vernon Charles AKES RAAF aged 23 - died of injuries

CREW
Pilot Officer Henry Barrymore ROWLAND RAAF aged 22 – killed
Sergeant Eric Ritchie BOWMAN aged 25 – died of injuries
Sergeant Gerald Harry SAVOY aged 21 - killed
Sergeant Reginald John CLARK aged 21 - died of injuries
Sergeant Edward Cameron WELSH aged 34 - killed
Corporal Sam Hawley ATKINSON aged 18 - injured
Corporal John William DAWSON aged 28 - injured
Corporal Jack MAINWARING aged 19 - injured

In 1941 the Royal Air Force began to see the introduction of the first of the new four-engined heavy bombers, such as the Short Stirling and Handley-Page Halifax. As a result, it needed to provide existing aircrews, who had been used to flying twin-engined aircraft such as the Vickers Wellington, with practical experience on the new aircraft. In October 1941 No.26 Conversion Flight was formed at RAF Waterbeach in Cambridgeshire using personnel from No.7 Squadron and eight Short Stirlings. Eventually, in January 1942, No.26 CF combined with No.106 CF to form No.1651 Heavy Conversion Unit. As the war progressed the HCUs, as they were known, would eventually become the last staging post for many new crews as the they entered operational service.

Bedfordshire [63]

Losses, as the result of accidents, were significantly high but the HCUs provided invaluable knowledge for aircrews and remained in existence throughout the war.

Left: the pilot of Stirling N6066, Sgt Vernon Akes.

On Christmas Eve 1941 a Short Stirling of No.26 Conversion Flight took off from RAF Waterbeach to carry out local flying practice. At the controls were two young Australians, Sergeant Vernon Akes, from Rosewood, Queensland and Pilot Officer Henry Rowland, of Warwick, Queensland. Akes and Rowland had both joined the Royal Australian Air Force in 1940 and were in the process of completing their conversion training on the newly acquired heavy bomber before returning to No.15 Squadron for operations. During what was to be a short routine flight the pilot opted to undertake some low level flying, which appears to have been an act of youthful exuberance, and was not something he was authorised to do. As the massive aircraft passed over West End Farm, Kempston, it struck a tall tree, went out of control and slammed into the ground. P/O Rowland, Sgt Savoy and Sgt Welsh all perished in the crash. The remainder of those onboard were injured and were taken to the County Hospital in Bedford where Sgt Akes, Sgt Bowman and Sgt Clark later died as a result of their injuries. The three corporals, who were training to be flight engineers, all recovered from their injuries and eventually all returned to flying duties.

Right: Stirling N6069 which rolled off the production line two airframes after N6066. These aircraft are from 1651 HCU which was formed from 26 Conversion Flight.

Below Right: The Court of Enquiry summary.

The Fate of the Survivors

Sadly, all three survivors from the crash were to lose their lives whilst serving with Bomber Command in 1942. Jack Mainwaring went missing on 2nd June whilst serving with No.218 Squadron, Sam Hawley went missing on 16th September whilst still serving with No.15 Squadron and John Dawson went missing on 1st October whilst also serving with No.218 Squadron.

Sgt Vernon Akes and Sergeant Edward Welsh are buried in the St. Margaret & All Saints Churchyard, Wyton, Cambridgeshire. P/O Henry Rowland is buried

CHRISTMAS EVE CRASH IN KEMPSTON

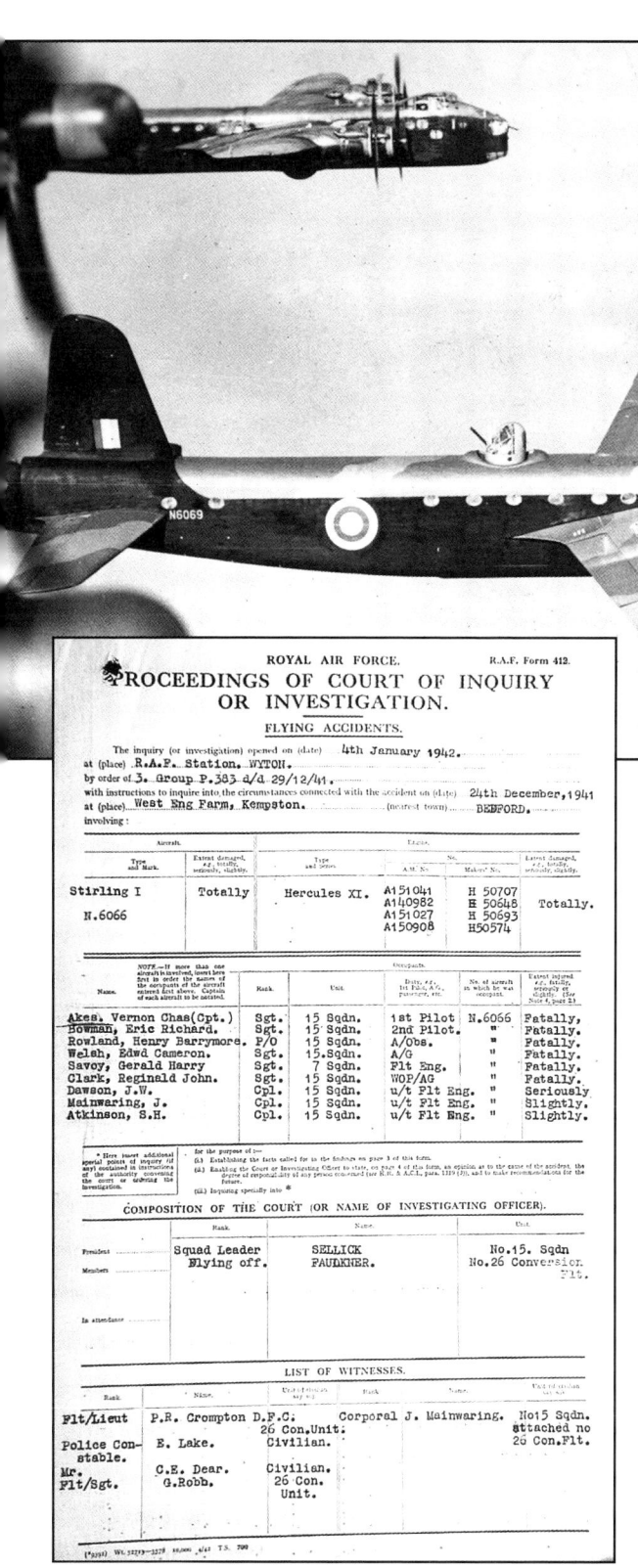

ROYAL AIR FORCE. R.A.F. Form 412.
PROCEEDINGS OF COURT OF INQUIRY OR INVESTIGATION.
FLYING ACCIDENTS.

The inquiry (or investigation) opened on (date) 4th January 1942.
at (place) R.A.F. Station, WYTON.
by order of 3 Group P.383 d/d 29/12/41.
with instructions to inquire into the circumstances connected with the accident on (date) 24th December, 1941
at (place) West End Farm, Kempston. (nearest town) BEDFORD.
involving :

Aircraft			Losses		
Type and Mark	Extent damaged, e.g. totally, seriously, slightly	Type and Series	A.M. No.	Maker's No.	Extent damaged, e.g. totally, seriously, slightly
Stirling I N.6066	Totally	Hercules XI.	A151041 A140982 A151027 A150908	H 50707 H 50648 H 50693 H50574	Totally.

Name	Rank	Unit	Duty, e.g. 1st Pilot, A/G, passenger, etc.	No. of aircraft in which he was occupant	Extent injured e.g. fatally, seriously or slightly.
Akes, Vernon Chas (Cpt.)	Sgt.	15 Sqdn.	1st Pilot	N.6066	Fatally.
Bowman, Eric Richard.	Sgt.	15 Sqdn.	2nd Pilot.	"	Fatally.
Rowland, Henry Barrymore.	P/O	15 Sqdn.	A/Obs.	"	Fatally.
Welsh, Edwd Cameron.	Sgt.	15.Sqdn.	A/G	"	Fatally.
Savoy, Gerald Harry	Sgt.	7 Sqdn.	Flt Eng.	"	Fatally.
Clark, Reginald John.	Sgt.	15 Sqdn.	WOP/AG	"	Fatally.
Dawson, J.W.	Cpl.	15 Sqdn.	u/t Flt Eng.	"	Seriously
Mainwaring, J.	Cpl.	15 Sqdn.	u/t Flt Eng.	"	Slightly.
Atkinson, S.H.	Cpl.	15 Sqdn.	u/t Flt Eng.	"	Slightly.

COMPOSITION OF THE COURT (OR NAME OF INVESTIGATING OFFICER).

	Rank	Name	Unit
President	Squad Leader	SELLICK	No.15. Sqdn
Members	Flying off.	FAULKNER.	No. 26 Conversion Flt.

LIST OF WITNESSES.

Rank	Name	Unit
Flt/Lieut	P.R. Crompton D.F.C.	26 Con.Unit.
Police Constable.	E. Lake.	Civilian.
Mr.	C.E. Dear.	Civilian.
Flt/Sgt.	G. Robb.	26 Con. Unit.
	Corporal J. Mainwaring.	No15 Sqdn. attached no 26 Con.Flt.

in the St. Peter Churchyard, Slinfold, Sussex. Sgt Reginald Clark is buried in the St. George Churchyard, Portland, Dorset. Sgt Eric Bowman is buried in the Bangor Cemetery, Co. Down, Northern Ireland. His brother Geoffrey Alexander Bowman was killed in May 1944 whilst serving with No.53 Squadron. Sgt Gerald Savoy is buried in the Waterbeach Cemetery, Cambridgeshire. His brother Derrick William Savoy was killed in September 1943 whilst serving with 106 Squadron.

1942

THE DESERT AIR FORCE COLLIDE OVER BEDFORD

In October 1942 the 81st Fighter Group was preparing to take part in Operation Torch, the invasion of North Africa, as part of the US 12th Air Force. The Air Echelon arrived in the UK from Muroc Airfield, California and was based at RAF Kirton-in-Lindsey until the end of December where they flew Bell P-39 Airacobras. Whilst the group were in transit they were temporarily attached to the 8th USAAF. During their short stay in the UK they undertook a series of training and exercise flights in preparation for combat in the desert theatre, including mock 'dog fights'. On 23rd December two pilots, 2/Lt Ernest J Sharp of Douglas County, Oregan, and 2/Lt Melvin J Welch of Buchanan County, Missouri, took off from RAF Kirton-in-Lindsey to take part in a combat training exercise. A short while after leaving the ground the aircraft were seen over Bedford and appeared to be 'chasing each other', at which point they collided in mid-air and crashed. One fell on a railway embankment along the Ampthill Road and the other one came down on a bungalow in Miller Road. Both pilots were

23rd December 1942

LOCATION
Miller Road, Bedford

TYPE
Bell P-39 Airacobra

SERIAL No.
BX163 (2/Lt Sharp)

PILOT
2nd Lieutenant Ernest J SHARP
aged 26 - killed
2nd Lieutenant Melvin J WELCH
aged 26 - killed

CIVILIAN
Mrs Edith Agnes HUDSON
aged 28 - killed

Above: Men of the 81st Fighter Group pose with their P-39s.

killed. Several reports indicate that there was a civilian casualty but, in fact, there were two. One was a four year-old boy and the other was 28 year-old Helen Hudson who was the wife of George Arthur Hudson, of 2 Miller Close. With the lack of detail available it is reasonable to assume that the young boy who was injured was probably the couple's son.

An Eye Witness

Another pilot from the group, John L Wortham, witnessed an accident on 23rd December but his version of events, shown below, varies to those reported from other sources.

"Our planes, having been equipped with belly tanks, and flight tested, took off for the White Cliffs of Dover, the jumping off place for North Africa. There were 100 planes arranged in flights of four. From the position I was flying I could see most of the other planes. There were several hazards that would create problems for us. One of course was the other planes. The second was the large number of balloons anchored around the urban centers. The third was the low ceiling under which we were flying. The balloons were avoided without mishap. The low ceiling did provide a problem. While flying about 100 feet off the ground in close formation we found ourselves enveloped by clouds. I could not see any of the planes nor the ground below me. Fortunately the cloud was quite small and I soon found myself out of the fog with a ceiling of about 400 feet. All of the planes were still in front of me. I heaved a sigh of relief and began to relax. We were only 45 minutes away from our destination. My feeling of optimism was a little premature. About ten minutes later I saw a flight of two planes changing position. They were moving beneath another flight. I shall never forget the scene that I was to witness. The propeller of one of the planes struck the 500 gallon belly tank of the plane under which it was attempting to fly. An explosion occurred and I saw a big fire ball. The two planes slowly spun toward the ground. Neither pilot had an opportunity to bailout. It was not a pleasant way to end 1942 nor to start the journey to North Africa."

The Crash Site Today

One can visit both crash sites today but you are unlikely to find any relics, as most of the wreckage was removed by the Salvage and Recovery teams of the USAAF. Sadly, there are also no memorials to those who perished on that day, so long ago. Ernest Sharp is buried at the American Military Cemetery, Cambridge. Melvin Welch was originally buried in Brookwood Cemetery but his body was repatriated to Missouri after the war.

The Bell P-39 Airacobra was an unusual aircraft in that the engine was positioned behind the pilot in the middle of the fuselage. Note the external belly fuel tank which is mentioned in the crash report.

1943

TWO NIGHTFIGHTERS IN TWO NIGHTS

15th April 1943

LOCATION
Putnoe Wood

TYPE
Bristol Beaufighter IF

SERIAL No.
R2098

UNIT
415th Night Fighter Squadron, United States Army Air Force

PILOT
Flight Officer Fred L DYER aged 22 - killed

When the USAAF formed its first radar-equipped night fighter squadron in January 1943, the only American night fighter available was the makeshift Douglas P-70, a modified A-20 bomber, using the U.S. version of the Mk IV radar. After initial training in the P-70, the first USAAF night fighter squadrons went to war in the more capable, British, Beaufighter. The 414th, 415th, 416th and 417th Night Fighter Squadrons received more than 100 'reverse Lend-Lease' Beaufighters. Some of the pilots underwent conversion training at 51 OTU operating from Twinwood Farm before they began operations in the Mediterranean. In April 1943 two accidents occurred within two nights that took the lives of the American pilots.

Much of the content of this publication centres upon the final fate of an aircraft and its crew. Sometimes, however, the aircraft itself has a much greater story to tell. Such is the case with Bristol Beaufighter R2098. Her final attachment was to the 415th Night Fighter Squadron of the United States Army Air Corps. The squadron became one of the first graduates of the hastily organised training programme in Orlando, having previously flown P-70s. After its transfer to England in late March 1943, the squadron gained additional training from experienced British units. While in the UK, the pilots practised night flying in Blenheims left over from the Battle of Britain before converting to Beaufighters and giving up the P-70s in

Above: An early Beaufighter MkI in RAF service. Many of these aircraft were subsequently transferred to the USAAF in a 'reverse lend lease' deal.

Opposite page: Another early Beaufighter, T4638, from the same batch as the one that crashed at Putnoe Woods.

which they had trained in the States. The P-70 had proved too slow in climbing to operational altitudes and performed poorly at high altitudes. Several veteran U.S. pilots already flying with the RAF joined the 414th and 415th before they moved to North Africa for combat in July 1943. On 15th April 1943 R2098 was on a training flight piloted by Flight Officer Fred L Dyer (USAAF) of 415 Fighter Squadron when it crashed into Putnoe Woods, North of Bedford.

A Distinguished and Dubious Career

It was in this aircraft, on 19th November 1940, that John 'Cats Eyes' Cunningham and his radar operator John Phillipson made the first successful night fighter interception of an enemy aircraft by a Beaufighter. Then, on 11th May 1941, P/O František Behal, a Czech pilot of No.1 Fighter Squadron, was flying Hurricane Mk.IIA, Z2921 on night fighter operations. After claiming the destruction of a Heinkel He111 he was shot down at 00.50 hours in Selsdon Park, Surrey, and killed. Initially, it was believed that he was shot down by Oblt Boxhammer, but it seems to be more likely that he was, in fact, a victim of friendly fire and was shot down by F/O Edward D. Crew DFC and R/O Sgt Norman Guthrie of No. 604 Squadron, flying in their Beaufighter R2098. P/O Behal is buried in St.Luke's Graveyard, Whyteleafe, Surrey.

Fred Dyer is buried in the Wesley Chapel United Methodist Church Cemetery, Villa Rica, Carroll County, Georgia, USA.

Willard Gress was born in Glendive, Montana and move to Tacoma, Washington in 1924. After graduating from Lincoln High School he enrolled at Washington State College where he enlisted in the USAAF. He was commissioned as a 2nd Lieutenant at the Army Flying School in Victorville, California and was promoted to 1st Lieutenant following his arrival in the UK, with the 415th Fighter Squadron.

17th April 1943

LOCATION
RAF Twinwoods

TYPE
Bristol Beaufighter IF

SERIAL No.
T4646

UNIT
415th Night Fighter Squadron, 8th United States Army Air Force

PILOT
2nd Lieutenant Willard James GRESS aged 23 - killed

On 17th April 1943 Gress was at RAF Twinwoods where he was undertaking conversion training on the Bristol Beaufighter. He was tasked with performing a short take-off and landing circuit of the airfield and, shortly after leaving the ground, was coming into land when the Beaufighter struck a tree at the edge of the airfield. A short accident report found that Gress had failed to take overshoot action by not placing his props in fine pitch on approach to the ground. He was killed instantly in the resulting crash. Although he was originally buried in Brookwood Cemetery, Surrey, his body was later re-interred in Mountain View Cemetery, Auburn, King County, Washington, USA and his name is recorded on the Washington State Roll of Honor.

THUNDERBOLTS OVER EATON FORD

The 78th Fighter Group was activated in 1942 and initially trained for combat with P-38s. After serving as part of the West Coast Air Defense Organization in the USA the group moved to England in November 1942 where it was assigned to Eighth Air Force and based at RAF Goxhill. The Group consisted of the following squadrons, 82nd Fighter Squadron (MX), 83rd Fighter Squadron (HL) and 84th Fighter Squadron (WZ) and were distinguished by a black/white chequerboard pattern on their noses. The first draft of pilots were assigned to Twelfth Air Force in February 1943 for service in the North African campaign and the Group was re-equipped with P-47 Thunderbolts in April 1943 after which it moved to RAF Duxford in Cambridgeshire.

Training began in earnest on the new fighter for the latest draft of pilots and on 15th April 1943 when two Thunderbolts of the 83rd Fighter Squadron took off from Duxford on a combat training mission using camera guns. Just north of RAF Tempsford the two aircraft collided in mid-air. The first aircraft, 41-6241, piloted by 2/Lt Leroy V Dodd, crashed to the ground at Eaton Ford and the pilot was killed. The other aircraft crashed at a railway bridge near St.Neots but the pilot, F/O Major C Leach, survived. After recovering from the accident Leach returned to his unit and went on to fly many missions escorting B-17 and B-24 bombers as they attacked industries, submarine yards and docks, V-weapon sites, and other targets on the Continent. The unit also strafed and dive-bombed airfields, trains, vehicles, barges, tugs, canal locks, barracks, and troops. Major Leach was shot down in combat with FW190s on 5th January 1944 and again

---

15th April 1943

LOCATION
Eaton Ford

TYPE
Republic P-47C Thunderbolt

SERIAL No.
41-6241 HL*W & 41-6272

UNIT
83rd Fighter Squadron,
78th Fighter Group
8th United States Army Air Force

PILOT(S)
2nd Lieutenant Leroy V DODD aged 22 - killed
Flight Officer Major C LEACH survived

survived the crash and initial capture. He is believed to have been captured and killed at a later date, possibly by German troops, and is officially recorded as Missing in Action on 6th January 1945. Major Leach is commemorated on the Wall of the Missing at Cambridge Military Cemetery. He was awarded the Distinguished Flying Cross, Air Medal with 3 Oak Leaf Clusters and the Purple Heart.

The body of Leroy Dodd was originally buried in the American Military Cemetery in Cambridge, but after the war was re-interned in the Hartford Memorial Cemetery, Sebastian County, Arkansas, USA.

Below: A Republic P-47C Thunderbolt over England.

AN UNUSUAL BIRD AT WHIPSNADE

Research shows that none of the operational units of the USAAF that were sent to the UK were equipped with P-40s. However, fifteen of this type of aircraft arrived in March 1943 for transfer elsewhere and two P-40Es were acquired by VIII Bomber Command and used for fast liaison by the Headquarters Flight. One of these, serial number 41-36028, crashed near Berkhamsted on 23rd Sept 1942 killing the pilot, Captain William L. Knowles. The other, serial number 41-35934, remained with VIII Bomber Command until 9th October 1943.

The pilot

Glenn Hagenbuch joined the U.S. Army Air Corps on 10th September 1940 and, following his training, was assigned as a pilot in the 427th Bomber Squadron, 303rd Bomb Group, joining his unit on 1st May 1942 at Gowen Field, Boise, Idaho. He was assigned a crew in August 1942 at Biggs Field, El Paso, Texas and promoted to Captain on 2nd September of that year. A few weeks later Hagenbuch and his crew were part of the Air Echelon that undertook the long haul flight from the United States to RAF Molesworth in Huntingdonshire in preparation for combat duties. Their aircraft, B-17F 41-24619 S-for-Sugar, was nicknamed 'Good Ole 619' and its Bugs Bunny nose art was later adopted as the 427th Bomber Squadron insignia. On 3rd January 1943, mission No.9 to St. Nazaire, France the B-17 in which Squadron Commander, Major Sheridan, was flying blew up in mid-air over the target killing the entire crew. Captain Hagenbuch was later appointed the 427th Bomb Squadron CO. On 27th February 1943 a little known United Press journalist, Walter Cronkite, wrote an article titled 'Bombs Fall Amid Fight High In Air' in which he describes an attack by the 8th Air Force on the German naval base at Wilhelmshaven.

9th October 1943

LOCATION
Whipsnade, Bedfordshire

TYPE
Curtiss P-40E Warhawk

SERIAL No.
41-35934

UNIT
Headquarters.
8th United States Army Air Force

PILOT
Major Glenn E HAGENBUCH
aged 24 - killed

Above: Glenn Hagenbuch (back row far left) and his crew with their B-17, April 1943.

Below: The wreckage of the P-40 in which Hagenbuch was killed lies in the front garden of the Land Army Hostel in Whipsnade.

In this article he names the crew of the aircraft in which he was flying including the skipper, Captain Glenn E Hagenbuch. A few months later, on 29th June 1943, Cronkite again quoted Hagenbuch in an article on the attack of the French town of Le Roger. Hagenbuch was promoted to Major on 30th March 1943 and after completing his 25th combat mission on 29th June 1943, Hagenbuch was made part of a special mission to North Africa. Upon his return to England he was transferred to the VIII Bomber Command Headquarters in High Wycombe.

The Accident

At 10.10am on 9th October 1943 Major Hagenbuch took off from Bovingdon airfield on a short liaison flight, piloting Curtiss P-40 Warhawk 41-35934. There are no records that can identify what happened after he left the ground, but a short while after taking off his aircraft spun into the ground in the front garden of the Land Army Hostel opposite the Chequers Public House in Whipsnade. Initially, he was buried in plot K-8-13 at Brookwood Military Cemetery, but was later reburied in Illinois. He was awarded the Silver Star Medal on 13 May 1943 and an Oak Leaf Cluster to this medal on 26 September 1943.

BLACK THURSDAY - A HELL'S ANGEL IN THE GARDEN

One of the legendary units of the Eighth Air Force that served in England during WW2 was the 303rd Bomb Group (Heavy). The ground echelon left the USA aboard the Queen Mary on the 23rd August 1942 and finally arrived at Molesworth, Huntingdonshire on 9th September. The air echelon, comprising of the 358th, 359th, 360th and 427th Bomb Squadrons, arrived in late October, and the stage was set for their entrance into combat. Over the coming months and years the unit, nicknamed 'Hell's Angels', would fly a total of 364 Operational Missions across Nazi held Europe. One of the aircraft that served with the group was a Boeing B-17F Flying Fortress with the serial number 42-5482. It was delivered to Cheyenne Airfield, a completion and modification centre for B-17 aircraft, on 15th December 1942 was assigned to the 359th Squadron on 6th March 1943 where it was given the squadron identification code BN*W and nicknamed 'Cat o' 9 tails'. This is the story of her service and final fate in a small Bedfordshire village, where she and her crew continue to be remembered to this day.

The 'Cat' flew her inaugural operational mission on 22nd March 1943 when her pilot, 1/Lt George J Oxrider, and his crew were tasked with attacking the docks at Wilhelmshaven, Germany. She returned her crew safely to Molesworth and although most of them went on to complete their combat tours of 25 missions, two were to later lose their lives. 1/Lt George Oxrider, her pilot, was killed on 9th April 1944 when the B-17 he was co-piloting was shot down off of the Danish coast. Before her demise the 'Cat o' 9 tails' was to become a veteran of 31 operational missions over occupied Europe. Her career saw her carry a number of different pilots and crews, some of whom were to lose their lives in other aircraft or on later operational and non-operational flights.

14th October 1943

LOCATION
170 High Street, Riseley

TYPE
Boeing B-17F Flying Fortress

SERIAL No.
45-5482 'Cat o'9 tails' BN-W

UNIT
359th Bomb Squadron, 303rd Bomb Group 'Hell's Angels'

PILOT
2nd Lieutenant Ambrosse P GRANT

CO PILOT
2nd Lieutenant Franklin C HALL

NAVIGATOR
2nd Lieutenant James F BERGER

BOMBARDIER
2nd Lieutenant Marion D BLACKBURN

RADIO OPERATOR
Technical Sergeant J SEXTON

TOP TURRET
Staff Sergeant Anthony J KUJALA

BALL TURRET
Staff Sergeant Chester PETROSKY

WAIST GUNNER
Staff Sergeant Woodrow L GREENLEE

WAIST GUNNER
Technical Sergeant Robert F JAQUEN

TAIL GUNNER
Staff Sergeant Francis D ANDERSON

Schweinfurt

In March 1943 the city of Schweinfurt had been selected as a target under the terms of Operation Pointblank, the Allied Combined Bomber Offensive, due to the fact that the factories there produced over 45% of German military ball bearing requirements. The plants were initially bombed on 17th August 1943 as part of a 'Double Strike' mission that proved to be the greatest air battle yet staged over the European continent. During this mission the 'Cat o' 9 tails' was flown by 1/Lt Victor J Loughnan and his crew and they, fortunately, managed to survive the ordeal. The period between the 8th and 14th October 1943, with its extremely bad weather and heavy bomber losses, became known as 'Black Week'. One of the targets during this period was again Schweinfurt, which was attacked on 14th October, now known as 'Black Thursday', by several Bomb Groups including the 303rd.

Mission 78

On 14th October 1943, in foul weather, 291 B-17 Flying Fortress bombers crossed the German border on a second mission to destroy the ball bearing plants at Schweinfurt. Amongst these was B-17F 'Cat o' 9 tails', piloted by 2/Lt Ambrose P Grant, who was flying her for the first time, loaded with three 1,000lb General Purpose bombs plus five M47A1 incendiaries. Grant and his crew, who had already flown four other combat missions in another B-17F nicknamed 'Miss Be Haven', were flying in the No.5 position of the low squadron. The weather hampered the bomber formations' rendezvous, and as a result the wrong formations were in the wrong position. Many of the American aircraft were spread out, offering little protection for each other and an obvious invitation for Luftwaffe fighters. The bomber escorts had just turned back for England, due to their shorter range, and as the formation reached their target area they were set upon by an estimated 1,100 enemy fighters and bombers firing cannon and large calibre rockets. The single engine FW190s and Bf109s made head on attacks in groups of four and slashed through the formation before they rolled and dived away to reform and attack again. As soon as they were gone the next group of four would begin their attack. The twin engined Bf110s and Junkers 88s preferred to attack with their large rockets from behind

Above: The Cat provides the backdrop for 1/Lt Victor Loughnan (back row far left) and his crew.

or beside the formation, out of the bombers' machine gun range. The rockets were large enough and slow enough to be clearly visible to the bomber crews who had no defense and simply had to watch as the rockets flew into the formation in search of a target. The Junkers and a few Stukas actually dropped air fused bombs from above which were timed to explode in the middle of the B-17 formation. Any bomber that was damaged and fell out of formation was immediately set upon by a swarm of fighters. Without the protection of the rest of the formation there was very little chance of survival. Each of the proceeding Bomb Groups dropped their payloads on the target area whilst an intense air battle went on around them. At 14.46 hours, just as the 303rd Bomb Group were about to take their turn, tragedy struck the 'Cat'. A 20mm shell exploded in the face of waist gunner, Staff Sergeant Woodrow 'Woody' Greenlee, seriously injuring his face and one eye. The radio operator, Technical Sergeant Ed Sexton, came to the aid of 'Woody' and bandaged his wounds. The intensity of the aerial onslaught prevented the other crew members from aiding Greenlee any further and he had to be left as the B-17 was rocked and buffeted by flak and gun fire. A few minutes after Greenlee was wounded the 'Cat' was set upon by two yellow nosed FW190s that approached her from the rear. Staff Sergeant Francis Anderson brought his tail guns to bear on the fast moving fighters and opened up at a distance of 600 to 700 yards. One of the fighters broke away but the other one kept coming in.

Anderson opened up his guns again, this time at a distance of less than 400 yards, and the fighter nosed up and seemed to hang in mid-air before spiralling down to the ground. The pilot was seen to bale out of his stricken aircraft and Anderson had his first confirmed kill.

The battle brought great loss to the bomber force with many aircraft being shot down or damaged. 'Cat o' 9 tails' had suffered the onslaught of a fighter attack and her rudder controls were shot away, the radio compass and other flight instruments were rendered inoperative and her waist gunner lay wounded on the floor of the ship. A hit on the port side had put one engine out, but this was not feathered until the bomber was out of German fighter range. Ambrose Grant carefully flew the battered B-17 by dead reckoning across the channel and brought it down through the overcast to look for RAF Molesworth, but found that the area was covered by fog. Staff Sergeant Robert Jaouen described what happened next, "We were struggling along, trying to keep the engines going. Several passes were made over the field, but we couldn't see the landing lights. Either they were obliterated by fog or they were not turned on, as there were reports that Germans might try to follow the planes in. As they were circling a break came in the clouds. We saw we were passing a church steeple and the pilot struggled to gain more altitude. Besides the crippled engines, we were running low on fuel, our control cables had been damaged, and keeping up altitude was near impossible, as was landing. Finally, after again struggling to gain altitude, Lieutenant Grant ordered the crew to bale out. First out was 'Woody' who was semi-conscious and had to be attached to a static line. Then I was ordered to follow him down. After leaving the chaotic conditions of the plane and the mission I never experienced such silence, before or since, as floating down through the clouds. I watched 'Woody' disappear into the fog and I was certain I knew where he was.

After landing in a cow pasture, I started looking for him in the opposite direction from where he had landed and I never did find him. He had landed, apparently revitalized by the cold air, not knowing if he was in England or Germany. The badly injured 'Woody' was trying to read his compass when he was found by a local farmer who took him on the back of a tractor to a nearby airbase. He remained in hospital until he was well enough to return to the USA where he underwent extensive plastic surgery. My landing was my first good break of the day, as I hit the mud near a gate where the cows had been standing, I couldn't have had a softer landing but I did have a little manure on my clothes. When I arrived at a farmhouse I found Chester Petrosky had entered a few minutes earlier. The people were very hospitable, but stayed a long ways away from me and I soon deduced that it was from the 'cow perfume' I had picked up on landing". The airmen were taken to a nearby hospital where they spent the night.

Right and below: Various views of the scattered wreckage of 'Cat o' 9 tails' near the village of Riseley.

BLACK THURSDAY - A HELL'S ANGEL IN THE GARDEN

1943

The 'Cat', now totally alone, flew on descending in a northerly direction, which took her back towards the Molesworth area. At about 6:40pm, as she continued to fly in a large circle, the aircraft used up her remaining fuel and went into a final shallow dive. The giant bomber, with her propellers wind-milling, was now headed directly towards Melchbourne Park on the outskirts of Riseley, where the U.S. Army had a series of bomb and chemical storage sites. The crewless plane skimmed across the tree tops of the woods, passed over the Sharnbrook Road and headed towards the cottage of the Gell family in Riseley High Street. It narrowly missed the twin chimney pots of a little cottage and entered the rear garden where the starboard wing smashed into a huge oak tree and was torn off. The aircraft was immediately thrown to the right and the outer port wing was torn off by an elm tree. The almost wingless fuselage was then sent hurtling through a gap in a hedge, where it is believed to have cart wheeled for several hundred yards before slamming into the ground.

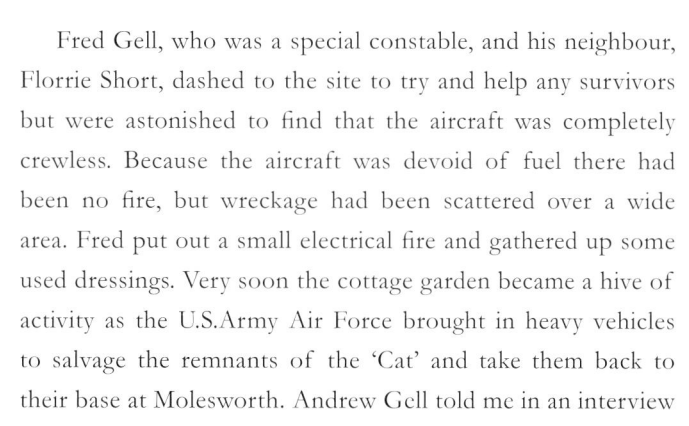

Left and below: More views of the scattered wreckage of 'Cat o' 9 tails' near the village of Riseley.

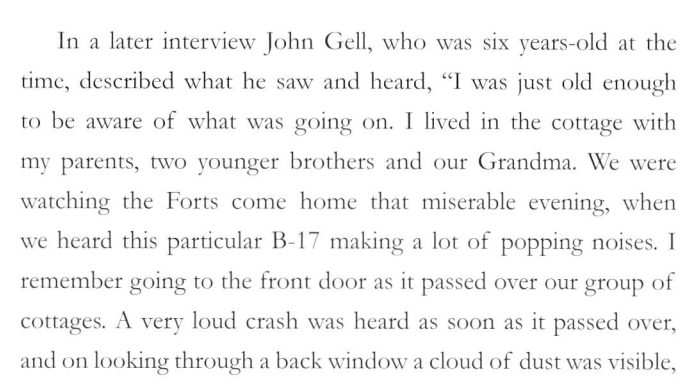

In a later interview John Gell, who was six years-old at the time, described what he saw and heard, "I was just old enough to be aware of what was going on. I lived in the cottage with my parents, two younger brothers and our Grandma. We were watching the Forts come home that miserable evening, when we heard this particular B-17 making a lot of popping noises. I remember going to the front door as it passed over our group of cottages. A very loud crash was heard as soon as it passed over, and on looking through a back window a cloud of dust was visible, with a large metal object about 80 yards away".

Fred Gell, who was a special constable, and his neighbour, Florrie Short, dashed to the site to try and help any survivors but were astonished to find that the aircraft was completely crewless. Because the aircraft was devoid of fuel there had been no fire, but wreckage had been scattered over a wide area. Fred put out a small electrical fire and gathered up some used dressings. Very soon the cottage garden became a hive of activity as the U.S.Army Air Force brought in heavy vehicles to salvage the remnants of the 'Cat' and take them back to their base at Molesworth. Andrew Gell told me in an interview that at first it was thought that the aircraft was nicknamed 'Betty My Honey' as this was the name painted on the outer starboard engine cowling. However, it soon became clear that the engine had been named by one of the ground crew and that the aircraft was actually called 'Cat o' 9 tails'. The recovery process caused considerable damage to the garden which, at the time, was being used to grow vegetables as part of the war effort. One of the propellers from the aircraft became buried in an area where Brussels sprouts were being grown. It is uncertain if this was an accident or if it was a deliberate act by Fred Gell, who simply wanted a souvenir from the accident. He retained the propeller for many years and eventually his son, John, restored it and it is now proudly displayed at the crash site by brothers Andrew and Nigel Gell.

The Crew – Beyond The Crash

When the final aircraft landed from that day's operation the toll amounted to a loss of 82 bombers and 642 airmen who were either killed, captured or wounded. This made 14th October 1943 the worst day of the war for the US Eighth Air Force and was forever known as Black Thursday. Following their ordeal all the crew of the 'Cat o' 9 tails' later became members of the famous 'Caterpillar Club.' They went on to fly with 2/Lt Ambrose Grant in several other B-17s including 'The 8 Ball' and the 'Idaho Potato Peeler'. This was with the exception of Woodrow Greenlee whose flying career had come to an end. On 5th November 1943 their B-17 was on a mission to Gelsenkirchen when it fell out of formation while on the group bomb run after being hit by flak, which damaged an engine. The

Top: The cottage in Main Street that just escaped being hit by the crewless B-17.

Above: One of the souvenired and restored prop blades.

[84]   WAR TORN SKIES OF GREAT BRITAIN

B-17 trailed behind the formation after leaving the target area and was last seen under attack by Luftwaffe fighters about 40 miles from the enemy coast, where another engine was knocked out. The 'Idaho Potato Peeler' eventually crashed in the small village of Eouw in the Netherlands near Roosendaal, but not before the crew had, once again, taken to their 'chutes. T/Sgt Edward Sexton suffered a foot injury while preparing to exit thorough the waist door. An explosion under the aircraft had driven shrapnel into his foot. Sadly, Sgt Joseph J. Hauer, who had replaced Woodrow Greenlee, was killed when his parachute failed to open. The remaining crewmen made successful bail outs and were quickly rounded up by German soldiers who were waiting on the ground. The enlisted crewmen were taken to Stalag 17B where T/Sgt Sexton's swollen and infected foot was treated by a Polish PoW doctor, about three weeks after he had baled out. T/Sgt Robert F. Jaouen had been stood down on the Gelsenkirchen mission and went on to fly another 22 missions with other pilots before completing his combat tour on 8th June 1944.

The Crash Site Today

The precise location of the final resting place of 'Cat o' 9 tails' can still be found today in the small village of Riseley. Sadly, John Gell passed away in 2003, but the house continues to be owned by the Gell family and I was fortunate enough to be allowed access to the site. The easily identifiable scars still remain upon the oak tree at the rear of the garden and the area in which the 'Cat' came to rest can still be clearly identified in comparison with photographs taken of the devastating scene at the time. It should be remembered that any intended visit to the area requires the authority of the Gell family.

REMEMBRANCE DAY COLLISION OVER CRANFIELD

11th November 1943

LOCATION
Cranfield

TYPE	TYPE
Bristol Beaufighter	de Havilland Dominie
SERIAL No.	**SERIAL No.**
R2252	X7368
UNIT	**UNIT**
51 Operational Training Unit	51 Operational Training Unit
PILOT	**PILOT**
Flight Lieutenant Michael William KINMONTH DFC - aged 21 - killed	Flight Lieutenant Archibald Menzies FITZRANDOLPH aged 47 - killed
PASSENGER	**PASSENGER**
Sergeant Lionel Maxwell AMESBURY aged 25 - killed	Sergeant Eric POVEY aged 22 - killed
PASSENGER	**PASSENGER**
Corporal Jose Cecilla HAYES (WAAF) aged 22 - killed	Flight Lieutenant Ian Harper COURTNEY aged 32 - killed
	PASSENGER
	2nd Lieutenant Joe K PETERS USAAF aged 25 - killed
	PASSENGER
	2nd Lieutenant Max A SCHIENKER USAAF aged 23 - killed

Many of the accidents that occurred across the country during the Second World War were as a result of pilot error, brought about by a misjudgment when flying. One of the greatest dangers that flyers faced in those busy, and less regulated, wartime skies was that of mid-air collision. When such an accident occurred it could be a particularly needless loss of a working aircraft as well as valuable personnel. There were a number of mid-air collisions over RAF Cranfield during WW2. A notable collision occurred on Armistice Day 1943 when a de Havilland Dominie, a military version of the Dragon Rapide, and a Bristol Beaufighter Mk.IF, both of 51 OTU collided in the middle of the afternoon, resulting in a heavy loss of life.

An accident investigation determined the events that led to the loss of two aircraft and eight personnel, including two members of the American Army Air Force. A copy of the report, stored in the National Archives, is outlined below;

"At about 14.49 hrs. on the 11th November 1943 Dominie (X7368), piloted by F/Lt Fitzrandolph was returning to Cranfield from RAF Hucknall and was making a normal approach from the East on runway 26, having received permission to land by Radio Transmission. The Beaufighter (R2252), piloted by F/Lt M.W. Kinmonth arrived from Twinwoods at about the same time. The Beaufighter, which was not in communication with Flying Control at Cranfield, had been sent round again about two minutes previously by a red signal cartridge from the Airfield Controller for cutting in on another Beaufighter's approach in a dangerous manner. After completing a tight circuit, the Beaufighter turned towards the runway with undercarriage and flaps down in a steep banking turn, cutting in on the Dominie, which was now in a straight approach. The Airfield Controller, seeing that both aircraft were approaching to land, shone his red Aldis lamp at the Beaufighter to indicate that he should go round again. This warning was either ignored or not seen by the Beaufighter pilot. A dangerous situation had now arisen, and the Airfield Controller fired a red signal cartridge towards the Beaufighter; at the same time the Flying Control Officer gave instructions via radio to the Dominie to go round again. This instruction was not acknowledged. The Dominie opened up and started to make height in a gentle turning climb to port. The Beaufighter opened up also, but by reason of its attitude continued in a steep banking turn, and the two aircraft collided at a height of about 100', just outside the perimeter of the airfield. The Dominie hit the underside of the Beaufighter with its starboard wing. The Dominie disintegrated and caught fire, crashing in flames on the edge of the airfield. The Beaufighter went into a steep dive, and crashed at

the beginning of the runway in use, and caught fire on impact with the ground. All occupants of both aircraft were killed instantly with the exception of 2nd Lt Peters of the USAAF who died a few minutes later on the way to sick quarters."

Above:
A de Havilland Dominie.

Opposite Page:
A Beaufighter of an OTU comes into land. Note how the engines obscure the vision of the pilot from certain forward angles.

The Personnel

The crew of the Beaufighter were Flight Lieutenant Michael William Kinmonth, aged 21, of Mount Meirian, Co. Dublin, Eire and Flight Sergeant Lionel Maxwell Amesbury, aged 25, of Weston-super-Mare, Somerset. On 30th April 1943 F/Lt Kinmonth had been awarded the Distinguished Flying Cross. Unfortunately, the London Gazette incorrectly listed him as F/Lt Kinmouth and the citation reads as follows; "This officer has completed much operational flying at night, displaying great skill, courage and devotion to duty throughout. He has destroyed 5 enemy aircraft.". At the time of the award he was serving with No.89 Squadron in the Middle East and Mediterranean areas.

Tragically, the two-seat Beaufighter also had a young WAAF clerk aboard on a short 'joy ride' from RAF Twinwoods a few miles away. She was Corporal Jose Cecilia Hayes, aged 22, of Paddington, London. Her grave can be found, along with the pilot, among those of the RAF air and ground crews who are buried in the Cambridge City Cemetery. Flight Sergeant Amesbury is buried in Weston-super-Mare, Somerset. Onboard the Dominie were five airmen. The pilot, Flight Lieutenant Archibald Menzies Fitzrandolph, aged 47, and his passengers Flight Lieutenant Ian Haper Courtney, aged 32, Sergeant Eric Povey, aged 22, and Americans 2nd Lieutenant Max Schenker, aged 23, and 2nd Lieutenant Joe Peters aged 25. Sgt Povey is buried in his home town of Smethwick, Staffordshire. F/Lt Fitzrandolph and F/Lt Courtney are buried in the Cambridge City Cemetery. The two Americans were originally buried in the American Military Cemetery in Cambridge but were re-interred after the war. 2/Lt Schenker now lies buried in Cook County, Illinois. 2/Lt Peters is believed to have been reburied in Kansas.

The Crash Site Today

Both aircraft came down just within the barbed wire perimeter of the airfield next to Merchant Lane, Cranfield, at the end of a now disused runway. There is little to be seen from the tragic events of that day but one can imagine the wasp like hum of the Dominie as it approached the airfield and what the thoughts of those aboard must have been as the Beaufighter thundered into their path. Fortunately this was to be the last mid-air collision in the vicinity of Cranfield.

LIGHTNING STRIKES TWICE AND PILOT SURVIVES

Anthony Tinto was born in Westchester, New York, on 3rd September 1917 and joined the Air Corps on 15th July 1941, just prior to the USA entering the Second World War. On 10th December 1943 2/Lt Tinto took off from Nuthampstead at 13.15 hours to carry out a high altitude training flight. After reaching a height of 30,000 feet the port engine started to run away. Tinto coolly managed to bring the engine under control but it soon ran away again, and this time he could not get it back under control. Black smoke started to pour from the over revving engine and began to fill the cockpit. Tinto opted to bale out from the distressed aircraft which then crashed at Manor Farm, Wrestlingworth. This was not the only time that Tinto was involved in a crash with a P-38.

10th December 1943	
LOCATION	Manor Farm, Wrestlingworth
TYPE	Lockheed P-38H Lightning
SERIAL No.	42-67057
UNIT	338th Fighter Squadron 55th Fighter Group
PILOT	2nd Lieutenant Anthony J TINTO

On 13th April 1944 he was returning to Nuthampstead when his aircraft lost an engine on landing and flipped over, off the end of the runway. Tinto was injured on this occasion but again managed to survive the crash. 2/Lt Tinto was credited with the destruction of two Me109s in air combat during his time with the 55th Fighter Group. One on 24th February 1944, and a second on 11th June 1944 near Beauvais, France. Tinto survived his service in the USAAF and later lived in Culver City, California, where he passed away on the 19th June 1995.

Below: The P-38 42-67057 that crashed at Manor Farm.

1944

MYSTERY AT TETWORTH HALL - THE PERILS OF INTERNET RESEARCH

The essence of any historical research is to ensure that the facts are clearly and accurately recorded. The availability of internet forums, chat rooms and free website space has provided the masses with the opportunity to record their views, opinions and recollections of historical events for the consumption of anyone who chooses to enter a few simple words into an internet search engine. Sadly, some of this information is often distorted by well-intentioned but poorly informed individuals, which can lead to the creation of historical inaccuracies. Such is the case with two events that took place near Tetworth Hall during the Second World War. A simple internet search will provide the details of an accident that took place there in January 1944. However, the indications from a number of websites are that an aircraft crashed onto cottages at Tetworth Hall and a civilian was killed on the ground and several others injured. This is not the case. Equally, a further search will reveal how, in May 1944, a Mustang crashed onto a cottage at Tetworth Hall, killing a female civilian. This, too, is not factually correct and the two events have become blurred. I have, through the study of official records, established the facts of both incidents and have recorded them below in the hope that future generations will have a full and complete understanding of what took place.

On 8th January 1944 a four-engined Halifax of No.138 Special Duties Squadron, LK743, lifted into the night sky above RAF Tempsford bound for Belgium. On board were a crew of seven and at least five members of the Special Operations Executive including, Hector Goffin, Rene Michaux and Henri Verhaegen who were taking part in Operation Tybalt 3, an organisational mission to contact resistance groups in Belgium and bring them within SOE coordination. It is believed that the aircraft reached its first drop zone where the British agent Wilfred Waddington and the Belgian agent Philippe de Liederkerke left the plane before it turned for home with engine trouble. After nearly five hours at the controls the pilot, P/O Harry Kennedy, brought 'J for Johnny' back to the Tempsford circuit with his port-outer engine out of action and lined the aircraft up for a final approach. Coming in low, and overloaded with 10 on board, the massive aircraft could not clear a clump of trees and crashed onto Tetworth Hill where it burst into flames, killing all aboard.

The Agents
- **Henri Verhaegen**

Henri was a sergeant in the Belgian Army. He joined the SOE after his parents were sent to a German concentration camp, where his mother later died. After the completion of his training as a wireless operator he was given the codename

8th January 1944

LOCATION
Tetworth Hill, Bedfordshire

TYPE
Handley-Page Halifax Mk V

SERIAL No.
LK743 NF-J

UNIT
138 Squadron, Royal Air Force

PILOT
Pilot Officer Harry Murray KENNEDY aged 23 - killed

CREW
Sergeant Peter Sidney BARLOW (Air Gunner) aged 22 - killed
Flight Sergeant David Fisher DAVIES DFM (Air Gunner) aged 23 - killed
Sergeant Thomas Samuel HOWLETT (Flight Engineer) aged 22 - killed
Sergeant Victor Albert Edward THEEDOM (Navigator) aged 22 - killed
Sergeant Edwin THRIPP (Wireless Op / Gunner) aged 23 - killed
Sergeant Stanley WHITELEY (Air Bomber) aged 20 - killed

Sergeant R. HIERSAUX - Survived

Sergeant Hector GOFFIN Passenger aged 25 - killed

Sergeant Rene P E MICHAUX Passenger aged 21 - killed

Captain Henri Paul VERHAEGEN Passenger aged 21 – killed

Rhomboid and returned to Belgium in October 1941 with the well known SOE agent Jean Cassart. It seems that at the end of 1941 a courier, whose patriotism was undoubted but whose courage was poor, had been caught in the south of France carrying incriminating documents. He was brutally interrogated and gave up the names of Fernand and Jean Kerkhofs-Moens, who ran the courier service known as 'Zero', from a mezzanine floor of the Palace of the Count of Flanders, Place Royale. He also gave the names of Georges Leclercq, Andre Bernard and Henri Cauvin who ran the resistance group named 'Luc'. The man pretended that he would work for the Germans and rushed to Brussels to warn the men he had denounced. It was decided that Cassart and Verhaegen should return to London as soon as possible. Jean Mahieu, one of Cassart's trusted men, had a small Opel car, bearing registration plates of the Swedish consulate, which allowed it to move freely across the French/Belgian border. For several days, everyone waited at the Cafe Vonèche for the arrival of a Lysander which would pick up the two men and drop off vitally needed supplies. At seven o'clock in the evening of 6th December 1941 the group were anxiously listening for the personal messages transmitted by the BBC that contained coded instructions to resistance groups on the continent. They heard the first message which said 'The Eburones return' and finally the message announcing the pick-up which was 'The Mighty Have Menapii'.

The two men were taken by members of the group to a landing ground near Neufchateau, where lamps were being placed on the airstrip. At eleven o'clock, they abandoned their car in a small deserted road and made their way on foot. At this point, it is claimed, Jean Mahieu returned to the car as he had forgotten his ausweis. Jean Cassart and Henri Verhaegen continued on foot towards the landing area. The sound of a Lysander could now be heard and Henri Verhaegen whispered in Dutch "Ik hoor spreken" (I can hear it). Suddenly, the sound of motorcycles could also be heard from the surrounding area and members of the German Feldgendarme could be seen advancing towards the landing strip. The agents ran to the car but it was already in the hands of Feldgendarme. Then, Henry Verheagen who was near to the beacon lights, felt a gun pressed on his chest. The German policeman told him: "Light your lamp or I kill you."

Then the German, hearing that the Lysander was fast approaching, and fearing that the radio Verhaegan was carrying would be destroyed, tried to turn on the lamps himself. Verhaegen launched a strong kick in the belly of the German who bent towards the ground, as he did so Verhaegen snatched his gun and killed him. Two other Feldgendarme rushed to the rescue of their comrade and were slaughtered in their turn. At this point the Lysander landed, all lights on, and

Verhaegen and Cassart dashed across the airstrip to the waiting aircraft. The pilot, F/Lt Murphy had realised that something was wrong as he came into land and tried to save his comrades. A burst of machine gun rounds was fired at the men as they fled, with one of the rounds wounding Verhaegen and another striking the pilot in the neck. Although F/Lt Murphy managed to get the aircraft into the air and back to the UK the agents were forced to scramble away. Cassart was captured a few days later but managed to escape. Henri Verhaegen managed to get away and was again wounded on 8th February 1942, as he was being arrested. Fortunately, he managed to escape on the same day by killing his guard. He was later awarded the DCM and Croix de Guerre (Belgium) and promoted to the rank of Captain in the British Army. He was then given the codename Thersites and was preparing to return to Belgium when he was killed. Henri Verhaegen is buried at Mortseldorp, south of Antwerp.

- Rene Michaux

Rene came from the town of Tamines, and had been a member of the Belgian Army. He joined the Belgian Section of the SOE as a wireless operator and was given the codename Lucius.

- Hector Goffin

Hector came from the town of Chatelet, and had been a member of the Belgian Army. He joined the Belgian Section of the SOE as a wireless operator and was given the codename Fortinbras.

P/O Kennedy is buried in the Kirriemuir Cemetery, Angus, Scotland. Sgt Barlow is buried in the St John the Baptist Churchyard, Somersham, Cambridgeshire. F/Sgt Davies is buried in the Aberdare Cemetery, Glamorganshire and Sgt Howlett is buried in the Eastfield Cemetery, Peterborough.

The Mystery

Some reports and publications claim that the tenant of the cottage, Fred Gore, was killed in the crash and that his wife, Miriam, his sister-in-law and a certain Mr H.J. Waddington escaped. However, I established that the death certificate for Fred Gore showed that he was actually killed on 28th May 1944. The mystery is unravelled in the following paragraphs.

28th May 1944

LOCATION
Tetworth Hall

TYPE
de Havilland Mosquito

SERIAL No.
HX972

UNIT
60 Operational Training Unit Royal Air Force (or 2 GSU)

PILOT
Flight Lieutenant Keith Bewman COOLING RAAF aged 27 - killed

CREW
Flying Officer Jenneth Alfred HOWES (Navigator) aged 23 - killed

CIVILIANS
Mr Frederick GORE aged 33 - killed
Mrs Miriam GORE aged 33 - survived
Captain H.J. WADDINGTON - survived

On 28th May 1944, Mosquito HX972 took off detailed to carry out a low level cross-country flight. The aircraft was on the ninth leg of a low level cross country flight on a course from Braintree to St Neots power station approx 1.25 miles south of the town. In line with instructions he had received at the briefing the pilot, Australian F/Lt Keith Cooling, had altered course to port about 8 miles from St Neots, in order to strike the railway running north to the power station. Cooling, who had joined the Royal Australian Air Force in September 1940, brought the aircraft onto a course of 292 deg Mag, and a track of 284 deg true, and whilst he was altering course a low flying USAAF Mustang drew up alongside the Mosquito. The two aircraft, which witnesses believed may have been 'dogfighting', had been in this relative position for at least three miles when the Mosquito suddenly struck the top of an elm tree about 80 to 90 feet high. Amongst other damage, the starboard tail plane of the Mosquito came off, resulting in the complete loss of control by the pilot, and the aircraft crashed onto Tetworth Hall Cottage. Both the crew were killed and the occupant of the cottage, Frederick Oliver Gore, who was a 33 year-old market gardener's labourer. Mr. Gore had been in his bedroom at the time of the accident taking an afternoon nap. Two others were injured in the crash, Miriam Gore and H J Waddington. The accident was considered an error of judgement by the pilot whilst carrying out unauthorised manoeuvres.

F/Lt Keith Cooling and F/O Kenneth Howes are both buried in the Cambridge City Cemetery.

A THUNDERBOLT STRIKES AT PODINGTON

The loss of an aircraft, and a pilot's life, is often more keenly felt when it is as a result of a tragic accident. This is the case of 2/Lt Roy Wendell of the 84th Fighter Squadron. Wendell, who was born in South Forks, North Dakota, had only joined the squadron on 6th February 1944 and was in the process of completing his training before taking part in operational sorties over occupied Europe.

On 13th March 1944 Roy Wendell was at the controls of his P-47 Thunderbolt, nicknamed 'Isabel'. He took off from Duxford to carry out a local gun camera practice flight along with 2/Lt James O Patton Jnr, who was flying in Thunderbolt 41-6333. They had been in the air for almost an hour when they arrived over the airfield at RAF Podington, the home of the 92nd Bomb Group. Wendell and Patton began to 'buzz' the airfield and instigated an impromptu 'dogfight'. During this mock air battle Lt Patton closed the inter-cooler on his aircraft and, as he did so, appears to have pressed the fire button on his guns. 2/Lt Wendell's aircraft was tragically struck by the .50 calibre shells and dived into the ground in a field opposite, and slightly south of the HQ building, at Podington. Two haystacks that were nearby were set on fire and a water main was damaged. The aircraft was completely destroyed and the wreckage was removed a few days later by a USAAF transporter.

Today, the grave of 2/Lt Roy Wendell can be found in the American Military Cemetery in Cambridge, a poignant reminder to the exuberance of youth during wartime.

13th March 1944

LOCATION
Podington

TYPE
Republic P-47C Thunderbolt

SERIAL No.
41-6223 'Isabel'

UNIT
84th Fighter Squadron
78th Fighter Group
8th United States Army Air Force

PILOT
2nd Lieutenant Roy E WENDELL
aged 23 - killed

Opposite page: P-47 Thunderbolt 'Isabel' which was shot down in the tragic accident over Podington.

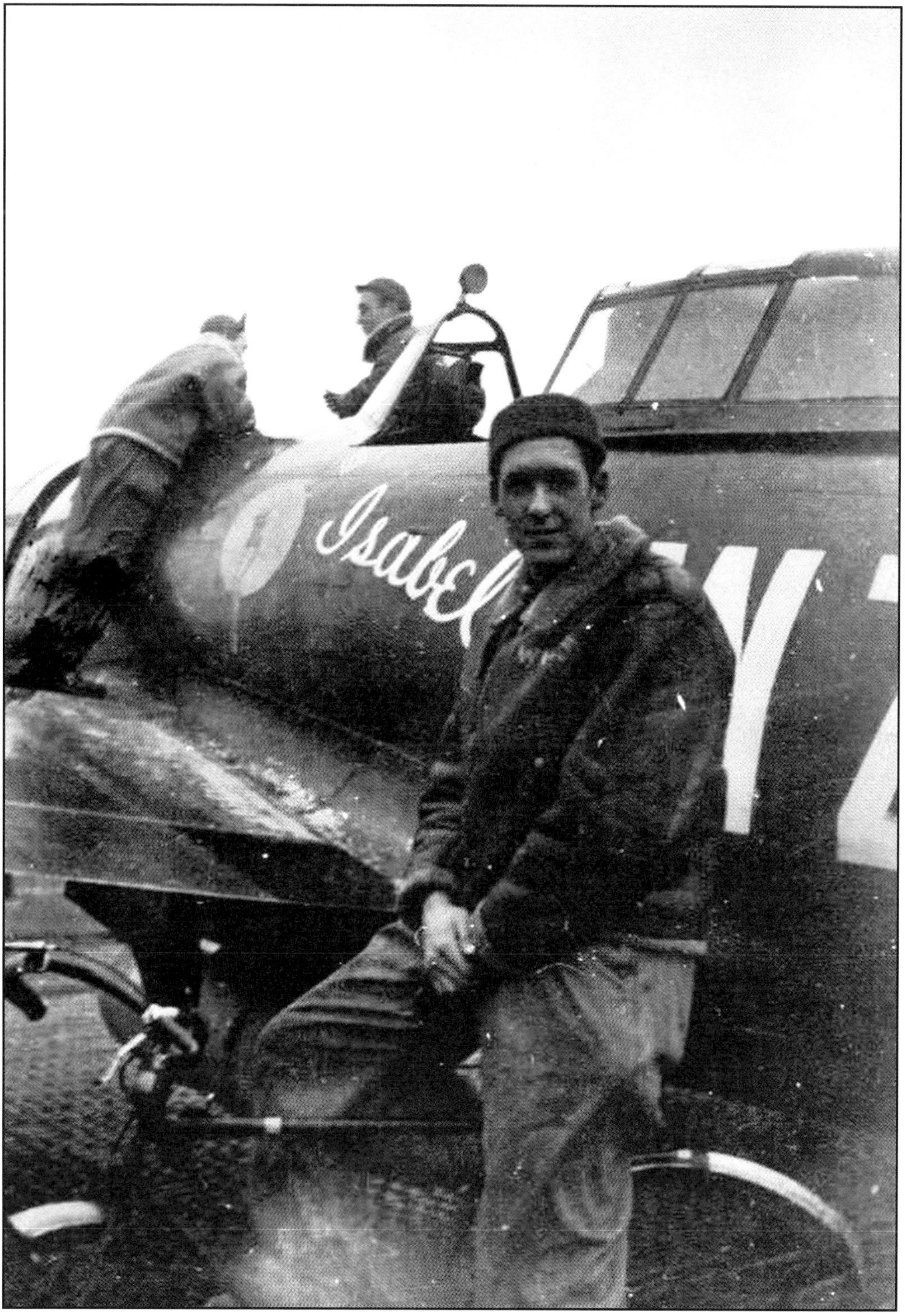
Isabel

A TRAGEDY AT YELDEN

The accident that befell B-17 42-97578 and the tragedy it brought to the Bedfordshire village of Yelden was the subject of long and intense research by the late William Donald of the 305th Bomb Group Memorial Association. In his book, 'John Burn Zero-One-Five', Bill Donald has extensively covered the incident and my thanks go to both his widow and to Ian White for their

24th March 1944

LOCATION
Yelden

TYPE
Boeing B-17G Flying Fortress

SERIAL No.
42-97578

UNIT
422 Bomb Squadron, 305th Bomb Group (Heavy)

PILOT
1st Lieutenant William D SELLERS - killed

CO-PILOT
1st Lieutenant Jack E GEORGE - killed

NAVIGATOR
1st Lieutenant Charles W LEAKE - killed

BOMBARDIER
2nd Lieutenant David A REMENTERIA aged 27 - killed

'MICKEY' OPERATOR
2nd Lieutenant Myer SILBER aged 24 - killed

ENGINEER
Technical Sergeant Donald C PARRISH aged 21 - killed

RADIO OPERATOR
Technical Sergeant Jesse J LEHR aged 22 - killed

WAIST GUNNER
Staff Sergeant Loyde J JUDD aged 28 - killed

BALL TURRET
Staff Sergeant Kenneth I MACE aged 21 - killed

TAIL GUNNER
Staff Sergeant Dale E RISHEL aged 21 - killed

ASSISTANT CREW CHIEF
Corporal Joseph N A GRUGNALE aged 21 - killed

Members of 876th chemical company who perished in their billet

Private Frank J AMATO	Aged 31	Buried in Illinois
Private First Class Arnold N CHIPOLETTI	Aged 31	Buried in Pennsylvania
Tec/4 Nils S JOHNSON	Aged 24	Believed to have been reinterred in Sweden
Private First Class Michael R ARATO	Aged 24	Buried in the American Military Cemetery, Cambridge
Tec/3 Edward W DELL		Buried in Nebraska
Corporal Robert P McLAIN		Buried in Indiana
Corporal Sebastoan J ATTILIO	Aged 27	Buried in New Jersey
Private William DICKERSON	Aged 23	Buried in Virginia

Civilians on the ground

Edwin Keith PHILLIPS	Aged 14
Monica Ruth PHILLIPS	Aged 4

co-operation during my research. The following entry is both an extract of the information from that publication combined with details from contemporary accident and incident reports.

On the night of the 23rd/24th March 1944 a radar equipped B-17G was due to be ferried from Chelveston to Deenethorpe from where it would lead an operational sortie to Frankfurt. One of the newly arrived crews, led by 1st Lieutenant William D Sellers, was assigned the task of ferrying the specially equipped bomber on the short flight where a more experienced crew would then take it over. Once it was established that there were no mechanical problems the aircraft was due to have its fuel tanks topped up in readiness for the operation. At the time the flight was due to take place repairs were being carried out on the main runway at Chelveston and the pilot was required to use the much shorter north-south runway. To make matters worse the engineers who were carrying out the repairs had left heavy equipment and materials at the south end of the runway, thereby shortening it even further.

At 00.45 hours 42-97578 took off from Chelveston, with 1/Lt William D Sellers at the controls. After only a very short run, the pilot pulled the heavily laden aircraft into a steep climb but it quickly began to lose speed. The aircraft, with its throttles pushed wide open, reached a height of about 200ft where it stalled and began to turn towards the little village of Yeldon. Sellers, struggling to maintain flying speed, brought the almost uncontrollable aircraft roaring towards a row of high elm trees where the bomber's right wing sliced through one of them. The doomed bomber then veered towards a U.S. Army barrack site at Yelden where it slammed into the earth. The plane, filled with a highly volatile payload, had ripped off the roof of the barrack and sprayed the sleeping occupants with burning fuel before smashing into Glebe Farm, instantly killing the entire crew as well as eight members of the 876th Chemical Company, who were billeted in the barracks. Sadly, the two children of farmhouse owners Walter and Hilda Phillips were also killed in the accident. Edwin, aged 14 and his 4 year-old sister, Monica, died as they slept. One of the first on the scene of devastation was Eddie Wahl, a 305th BG medic. He had just returned to the base after a night out when the accident happened. Along with a colleague, Glenn List, they entered the rear of the farmhouse where they found Walter Phillips kicking out a window in an effort to save his heavily pregnant wife. They managed to rescue the couple and get them to the Chelveston Base

Below: A 305th Bomb Group B-17G, identifiable by the group's 'triangle G' on the fin.

Hospital from where, after initial treatment, they were later transferred to a civilian hospital. Although he had suffered severe leg injuries, Walter Phillips eventually recovered from his wounds. Hilda Phillips gave birth to a son, Michael, a few weeks after the accident but almost lost her life during the process. She remained in hospital for almost a year but the emotional damage remained with her throughout the rest of her life. Michael felt that the devastating blow suffered by the family was made more bearable by the support shown by the members of the local community.

David Rementeria was born on 7th February 1916, in Hagerman, Idaho, the son of Mr. and Mrs. Benito Rementeria. He spent his childhood in Idaho and after he graduated from high school, attended Boise Junior College. David transferred to the University of Oregon where he studied for a law degree. He became a member of the Oregon Bar in June 1941 after which he moved to Canyon City where he formed a partnership with Roy Kilpatrick. David retired from practising law temporarily in June 1942 to take up his training in the Army Air Force. He married Grace Kingsley in Redding, California on 16th May 1943 and, soon after, was posted overseas. Before his death he had completed 17 missions over Europe, including several raids on Berlin.

1944

PLANE CRASHES ON VILLAGE NEAR RUSHDEN

Sleeping Children Killed—Crew and Others Perish

ASLEEP in a bungalow, two children were killed when a bomber crashed on a farm at Yelden, near Rushden, in darkness early on Friday. In the next room, their mother and father escaped miraculously from the rubble left by the crash, while fire completed the ruins of their home. The 'plane burst into flames and blew to pieces, about ten gallant airmen losing their lives.

Seven people who occupied a billet in the village, were killed when their building was shattered.

The children who perished were Keith Phillips, aged 14, and his sister, Monica, a schoolgirl, aged nearly five. Their parents are Mr. and Mrs. Walter Phillips who tenant Glebe Farm, a small farm of 50 or 60 acres, have lived at Yelden about ten years.

From the Rectory nearby the Rev. R. Paddick and his wife and Mrs. L. A. Cole were standing at the front door and saw the tragedy enacted.

"The 'plane," said Mrs. Cole to an "Evening Telegraph" reporter, "was making a terrific noise and appeared to circle over our house terribly low— we thought we could almost have touched it, though that is an exaggeration, of course.

"It came back and crashed into the farm bungalow. Immediately there were masses of flames everywhere; the 'plane must have broken up at once. A hayrick was also on fire.

"I dragged the Rector in and shut the door. We got into the study at the back of the house because we felt there would be an explosion, and then we felt we ought to go into the village. We could not get down our drive, so we scrambled through Mr. Hawkey's drive."

The church which stands just behind the shattered bungalow, had its windows blown out.

Left: The local news report showing the devastated bungalow near the church.
(via Ian White of the 305th BGMA)

Below: A view in the opposite direction showing the 876th Chemical Company's billets that were devastated by the crash. The only recognisable part of the aircraft is the charred tailfin in the centre of the photo.

Dale Rishel was born on 2nd August 1922 the son of Mrs. Bert Rishel of Uniontown, Pennsylvania. He entered service with the USAAF on 11th November 1942 and, after completing his training, embarked for England on 5th November 1943. Dale had completed 17 missions over Europe as a tail gunner before losing his life in the crash. His body was returned to the USA after WW2 as part of the repatriation programme. It is believed that Dale Rishell is buried in Uniontown, Pennsylvania.

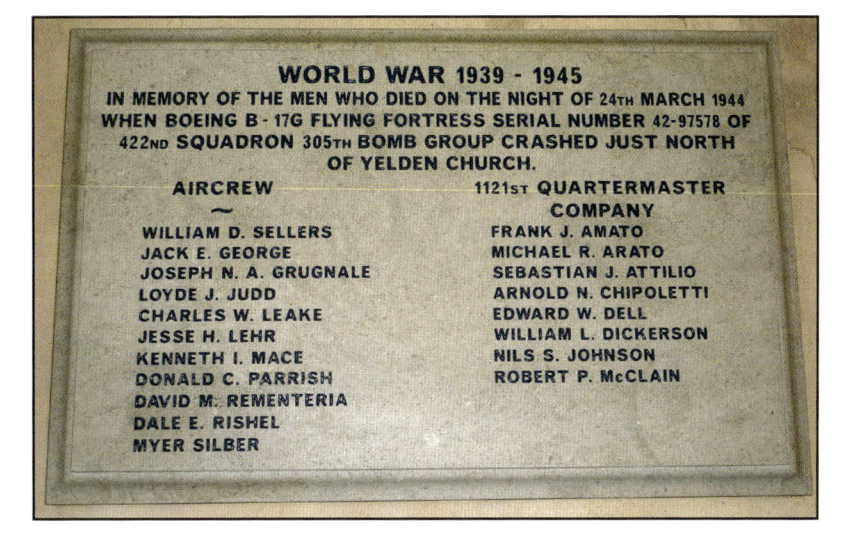

Right: A memorial plaque to the Americans who died in the crash can be found in the village church.

Below right: A street in Yelden named after the two young children who also died in the crash.

WORLD WAR 1939 - 1945
IN MEMORY OF THE MEN WHO DIED ON THE NIGHT OF 24TH MARCH 1944 WHEN BOEING B - 17G FLYING FORTRESS SERIAL NUMBER 42-97578 OF 422ND SQUADRON 305TH BOMB GROUP CRASHED JUST NORTH OF YELDEN CHURCH.

AIRCREW	1121ST QUARTERMASTER COMPANY
WILLIAM D. SELLERS	FRANK J. AMATO
JACK E. GEORGE	MICHAEL R. ARATO
JOSEPH N. A. GRUGNALE	SEBASTIAN J. ATTILIO
LOYDE J. JUDD	ARNOLD N. CHIPOLETTI
CHARLES W. LEAKE	EDWARD W. DELL
JESSE H. LEHR	WILLIAM L. DICKERSON
KENNETH I. MACE	NILS S. JOHNSON
DONALD C. PARRISH	ROBERT P. McCLAIN
DAVID M. REMENTERIA	
DALE E. RISHEL	
MYER SILBER	

The Crash Site Today

The location of the crash is in the area of Forge Gardens, Yelden. There is little evidence of the devastation and tragedy that occurred on that night but visitors to the nearby church will find a memorial plaque to those who perished which was unveiled in a formal ceremony in May 2009. The plaque was the idea of the 305th Bomb Group Memorial Association.

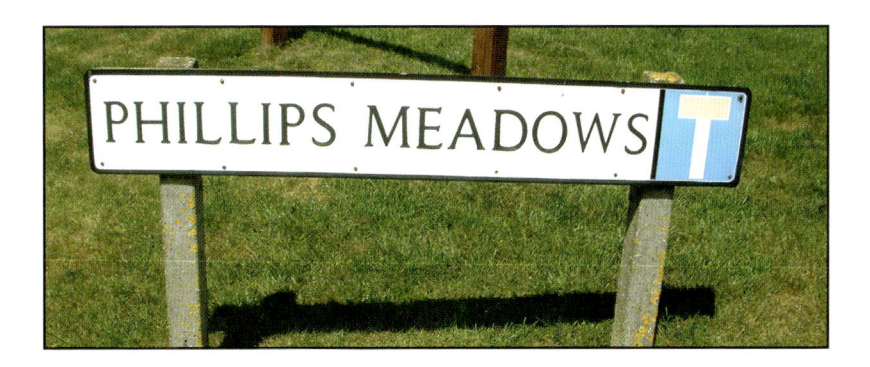

A RAIDER STRIKES AT LITTLE STAUGHTON

In the early hours of 23rd May 1944 Avro Anson LT476 took off from RAF Bicester to carry out a short navigational flight. At the controls was a young trainee pilot, Flying Officer Paul Davidson. His crew consisted of a staff navigator, W/O Lister, and two trainee navigators, F/Sgt Blyth and Sgt McConchie. The aircraft was flying at a height of about 2,000 feet and, in line with normal procedures at this time in the war, had its navigational lights switched on. When it was in the vicinity of Little Staughton airfield the calmness of the cockpit was suddenly shattered by a series of explosions. Cannon shells tore into the aircraft, one of which struck the pilot's back and exited out of his stomach. A second shell wounded F/Sgt Blyth in the thigh. The aircraft had been 'jumped' by an enemy raider, who was probably hanging around Little Staughton hoping to catch a returning Mosquito.

Below; The Avro Anson's flimsy wood and canvas fuselage offered the crew no protection against 20mm cannon shells.

23rd May 1944

LOCATION
Little Staughton

TYPE
Avro Anson

SERIAL No.
LT476

UNIT
13 Operational Training Unit

PILOT
Flying Officer Paul Alexander DAVIDSON aged 25 - died of wounds

CREW
Flight Sergeant R N BLYTH
Warrant Officer Paul G LISTER
Sergeant R F H McCONCHIE

With the pilot now seriously wounded the little Anson immediately went into a dive and W/O Lister, realising what was about to happen, quickly baled out of the stricken aircraft. However, Sgt McConchie, who was in the rear of the aircraft, came forward and assisted the injured pilot in bringing the aircraft under control. Together, the two brought the aircraft into Little Staughton where a successful landing was achieved. W/O Lister, who had baled out at a very low height, found that his parachute functioned perfectly and made a successful landing in a ploughed field. Sadly, P/O Davidson was unable to overcome his terrible injuries and died three days later as a result of his wounds. Today, his body lays buried in the Royal Air Force regional cemetery at Botley, Oxford.

THE PIGGYBACK RIDE OVER EATON SOCON

'Friendly Fire' is described as the *"inadvertent firing towards one's own or otherwise friendly forces while attempting to engage enemy forces, particularly where this results in injury or death"*. During the Second World War the incidents of 'friendly fire' were, unfortunately, numerous. One such incident is believed to have taken place on the night of 28th June 1944, when a Liberator of the 801st Bomb Group was undertaking a local training mission.

After taking off from Harrington in Northamptonshire for a cross-country training flight the aircraft was at a height of 2,000 feet and flying normally over Bedford when, at 02.35 hours, it began to shudder violently. An extensive fire immediately broke out in the fuselage and the pilot, 1/Lt Bill Huenekens, gave the order to bail out. The bombardier, 2/Lt Robert Sanders scrambled out of his position in the nose and moved up to the flight deck to retrieve his parachute. He found, to his horror, that the area was ablaze and his chute totally useless. He quickly returned to the nose where the navigator, 2/Lt Robert Callahan, was sat down by the escape hatch. An event then occurred which has made aviation history. Callahan knew that his comrade's life was in danger and there was only one course he could take to save his buddy. He told Sanders to straddle his back and wrap his arms around him tightly. He then slid out of the aircraft with Sanders holding on to his harness

---

28th June 1944

LOCATION
Staploe

TYPE
Consolidated Liberator B24H

SERIAL No.
43-95321 A -

UNIT
850th Bomb Squadron, 801st Bomb Group, United States Army Air Force

PILOT
1st Lieutenant William (Bill) Edgar HUENEKENS aged 27 - killed

CREW
Staff Sergeant Carl R. ADAMS Flight Engineer - killed
2nd Lieutenant Robert CALLAHAN navigator - injured
2nd Lieutenant John M CRONAN Co-pilot - killed
2nd Lieutenant Robert SANDERS Bombardier - injured
Sergeant Randall G SADLER Radio Operator - injured

straps. As soon as they left the aircraft and entered the slipstream Callahan pulled the rip cord and, with a jolt, the canopy opened. It was a tense moment, as Callahan feared that Sanders may be wrenched from his grip by the force of the chute opening. With great relief the two men remained entwined and Sanders manoeuvred himself to face Callahan as the two men miraculously floated earthwards, eventually ending up in a wheat field near Eaton Socon. The weight of the pair meant that the landing was a hard one, but they only suffered minor injuries, the worst being a broken ankle for Callahan. For his actions that night 2/Lt Robert Callahan was awarded the Silver Star. The incident was mentioned in the Stars and Stripes ETO issue of 13 July 1944. The radio operator, Sgt Randall Sadler, also managed to escape the stricken bomber but he had suffered severe burns.

The remainder of the crew were not so fortunate. The blazing aircraft was spotted by the Royal Observer Corps post at Eaton Socon and, after altering course and losing height, was seen to crash half a mile west of the observer post at Staploe. There is some indication that the aircraft floated gently, but uncontrollably, to the ground in a pinwheel fashion before hitting the ground. It showed little damage when rescue and salvage crews arrived but, sadly, the pilot, co-pilot and flight engineer had all been killed.

Above: 1/Lt Bill Huenekens and his crew.

At first it was thought that the Liberator had been attacked by a lone German raider but this has never been substantiated. Records show that there were no enemy aircraft in the area, and rumours quickly circulated that the night fighter was actually a Spitfire, but this possibility has never been substantiated either. Given the location of the crash site, less than 2 miles from Little Staughton, there is a possibility that the attacker may have been a Mosquito.

1/Lt William Huenekens and 2/Lt John Cronan are buried in the Cambridge American Cemetery. The pilot's name is also inscribed in the Memorial Church at Harvard University. The body of S/Sgt Carl Adams was originally buried in Cambridge, but was repatriated after the war and is believed to be buried in his home state of Iowa.

MISSION 512 - THE DEATH OF 'MISS LIBERTY BELLE'

The story of the last mission of Miss Liberty Belle begins in the early hours of 3rd August 1944. The aircraft, originally purchased with War Bonds from the citizens of Philadelphia, was prepared by her crew chief, M\Sgt John Van Camp, who had taken care of her throughout her 64 missions flying from Chelveston. This was to be her 65th operational flight, an assault on the Merkwiller oil refinery in the Alsace region of France, the last operational oil refinery on French soil to be fully under German control. Entitled Mission 512, it involved a strike by 106 B-17s of the 92nd, 305th and 306th Bomb Groups supported by the P-51D Mustangs of the 355th Fighter Group operating out of Steeple Morden.

After leaving the security of Chelveston airfield Miss Liberty Belle, piloted by 1st Lt Thomas Barnett, headed towards the now partly liberated European Continent. The mood aboard the aircraft must have been one of excitement and trepidation, as most of the crew were on their first operational mission. Sgt Charles Naden and Sgt Francis Schmidmeister had volunteered to fly as stand in gunners on other crews a few days earlier, so for them it was their second mission. The co-pilot, 2nd Lt Donald Morrill, was an experienced combatant and had already flown 28 missions. His job in the weeks prior to Mission 512 was to fly with rookie crews and check them out. This was a special day too for Morrill as he was celebrating his 21st birthday.

The outward leg of the journey took Miss Liberty Belle over the German town of Kaiserslautern and it was here that Flak knocked out one engine. Barnett and Morrill managed to maintain their position in the High Squadron and eventually bombed the target. The formation also became the target for German fighters of JG53 'Pik As' and attacks were made on the formation both during and after the bomb run. The German fighters were quickly engaged by the Mustangs of the 355th Fighter Group, who claim six enemy aircraft as destroyed. Sadly, during a break in the engagement, two P-51s, piloted by Lt Garlyn Hoffman and Lt Gilbert Patterson collided. Gilbert, flying in a P-51 nicknamed 'Sophia', was killed in the collision but Hoffman managed to bail out and was taken prisoner.

In the meantime, Miss Liberty Belle had pressed on and reached the Dutch coast where a second engine began to fail and eventually lost all power. They were now running on just two engines, a third barely ticking over. On

3rd August 1944

LOCATION
Wymington

TYPE
Boeing B-17 Flying Fortress

SERIAL No.
42-31255 XK-O 'Miss Liberty Belle'

UNIT
365th Bomb Squadron, 305th Bomb Group (Heavy), 8th United States Army Air Force

PILOT
1st Lieutenant Thomas D BARNETT
aged 23 - killed

CO-PILOT
2nd Lieutenant Donald D MORRILL
aged 21 - killed

NAVIGATOR
2nd Lieutenant John Lawrence RUTHERFORD - killed

BOMBARDIER
2nd Lieutenant Eugene James BONAS
aged 28 - killed

FLIGHT ENGINEER
Sergeant Floyd Wesley ROWE
aged 22 - survived

RADIO OPERATOR
Sergeant Donald Alvis McQUEARY
killed

BALL TURRET GUNNER
Sergeant Richard JASIONOWICZ
aged 19 - killed

WAIST GUNNER
Sergeant Francis J SCHMIDMEISTER
aged 19 - survived

TAIL GUNNER
Sergeant Charles Keith NADEN
aged 20 - killed

approaching Chelveston airfield a second plane, firing red flares, jumped ahead of them, forcing Miss Liberty Belle to go around for a second approach. At that moment one of the two remaining good engines began to overheat and eventually caught fire. Barnett and Morrill now pushed the throttles hard on the third lazy engine, and attempted to restart the dead fourth, in an effort to gain enough power to go around again.

The aircraft, now at less than 200 feet above the ground, banked around the village of Wymington. The Flying Fortress dropped until it was level with the village church steeple, just 125 feet high, forcing the massive bomber to slew to one side to avoid hitting it. In an amazing feat of airmanship, the pilots brought the plane back into level flight, just 60 feet above the ground and just clearing the thatched roofs below. Eye-witnesses saw and heard the plane as it passed overhead, shaking tea cups and plates on kitchen dressers as she headed over the village and back towards Chelveston. Then, in the last seconds, with one engine ablaze and two almost at a stop, Miss Liberty Belle struck one of several 60ft elm trees, ripping almost 8ft off of the top. The impact was taken between the co-pilot's position and number three engine, causing a further explosion. The plane was wrenched from the sky and crashed into a field beside the High Street, miraculously avoiding Manor Farm House and several cottages in that part of the village. Miss Liberty Belle then burst into flames with the ensuing fire consuming much of her fuselage and most of her crew, for whom their first operational flight had become their last.

Above: 'Miss Liberty Belle' waits for her previous crew to board.

The Rescue and the Aftermath

No sooner had Miss Liberty Belle struck the ground than eight villagers and a Czech soldier ran to the aid of the stricken crew. Leo Tobin, Victor Watts, Jack Lewis, Reginald Tobin, Richard Bristow, Herbert Fuller, George Dickerson, Michael Smith and Svob Harry Bartonieck reached the blazing wreck where they were faced with both devastation and danger. Hundreds of rounds of exploding .50 calibre ammunition and tracers filled the air, aviation flares had ignited, and the remaining fuel had spilled across the field, turning the B-17 into a blazing inferno.

These brave men first entered the tail section of the Miss Liberty Belle where they managed to pull the badly injured Frank Schmidmeister from his position. On the eve of his 20th birthday, Schmidmeister had survived the crash but suffered a severe fractured skull, lacerations to his brain and severe bruising all down his right side from head to toe. He spent five days in a coma, but went on to live until January 3rd 2005 when he passed away aged 80. Richard Jasionowicz, the ball turret gunner, was pulled unconscious from the wreck and was taken to hospital but died at 3am the following morning, having never regained consciousness. In the nose section the rescuers found the navigator, John Rutherford, he was semi-consciousness, and while he survived the initial crash, he died in an ambulance en route to hospital. Both the pilots had remained strapped in their seats. They were believed to be dead and the rescuers were unable to be reach them in ensuring fire. McQueary and Naden's bodies could not be reached and were badly burned and recovered after the fire was out.

Below: 2/Lt Eugene Bonas who was killed in the crash of 'Miss Liberty Belle'.

Eugene Bonas

The bombardier, Eugene Bonas, was pulled from the nose but was found to be dead. He was born in Prince Albert, Canada on the 22nd February 1916, the son of Charles and Mary Bonas. Although he was a British subject he was of German race. His parents were originally from North Dakota and Minnesota and they homesteaded in Saskatchewan, where they had six children. Their mother died in the flu pandemic in 1918. Many of these details are described on his Declaration of Intent, a document that is part of the U.S. naturalisation process. In August 1936 he left his home in Englefeld, Saskatchewan and travelled by bus to Regina and then onto Eastport, Idaho where he entered the United States. His father was already living there and it was thought there was no problem just crossing the border. He later found out that he had entered the country illegally. Along with his lawyer, he re-entered the country legally from Mexico and, in October 1937, now living and working in Los Angeles, applied for U.S. citizenship. Eventually, on 24th July 1942, his application was granted and, five days later, he enlisted in the U.S. Army Air Corps. Harry Bonas, Gene's brother, was a member of a top secret radio station in Greenland. All the radio communications, both friend and foe, were channeled through their station. Harry was on duty when the Miss Liberty Belle crashed and was the operator who decoded the message. He knew that was his little brother's aircraft and he knew there were survivors, but didn't know who they were until a couple of days later. I am indebted to Debi Bonas and her family for their help and support during my research.

Sergeant Floyd Rowe

Despite his sociable nature, Floyd Rowe never talked too much to his family about the day his damaged B-17 made a crash landing. Although he nearly lost an ear, he survived the accident after being thrown clear when Miss Liberty Belle struck the ground. At the time of the impact he had been crouched between the two pilots and was trying to help them maintain as much power as they could from their failing engines. He was thrown from the aircraft, landing some distance from the bulk of the wreckage with debris from the plane caught on his flight suit.

In 2000 a plaque was unveiled commemorating the bravery of the crewmen, as well as the townsfolk who rescued Rowe and Schmidmeister. At the memorial, also the site of the crash, Rowe was reacquainted with Michael Smith, who, aged 15, had assisted Rowe and also pulled deceased crewmembers from the wreckage. "Tears filled both their eyes," wrote Elizabeth, Rowe's daughter, "These two men, one a rescuer and one a survivor, finally met face to face after 56 years." Rowe and Smith retold the events of the crash to Elizabeth. "At times dad was shaking, he couldn't hold his hands still, I think he was reliving the whole thing over again," Elizabeth said. "Dad continued to tell how hard Morrill and Barnett worked to turn the plane away from the town . . . dad began to cry." "He broke down and sobbed, he couldn't believe he reacted that way and kept apologising. He had survivor's guilt. He kept saying, 'I shouldn't be alive, I should be with them' " Elizabeth said. Many townsfolk attended the memorial of the Miss Liberty Belle and thanked Rowe. "They were so thankful to the two pilots and the crew for the miracle they performed by turning that large plane, the Flying Fortress, away from their village," Elizabeth said. "It's an emotion that had to be experienced, by seeing the love and the sadness that these strangers have . . . for the one survivor that they could actually speak to. It is a feeling that I will treasure for the rest of my life."

Sadly, Floyd Rowe died of a stroke on 16th June 2008, aged 86 and is buried in the Northern California Veterans Cemetery, Igo, Shasta County, California, USA.

The Crash Site Today

Miss Liberty Belle made a shallow impact onto the pasture field which suggests that she was still under control when she hit the ground. This, combined with the ensuing fire, meant that a large majority of the wreckage was removed at the time of the accident. Nothing remains at the crash site apart from the occasional very small fragment. The reader should be reminded that the crash site is on private property and should not be visited without the landowner's permission. It should also be remembered that live ammunition may be found in the area of the crash and this should never be touched. If found, it should be reported to the landowner and the local police. Lastly, the crash site is a place where brave men died and it should be respected as such.

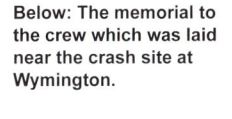

Below: The memorial to the crew which was laid near the crash site at Wymington.

The Memorial

The memorial, and its subsequent dedication in 2000, was arranged by Ian White and the late Bill Donald of the 305th Bomb Group Memorial Association. It can be found close to the crash site in Wymington village. I am most grateful for the assistance provided by Ian White during my research and for the information contained in Bill Donald's book 'John Burn Zero-One-Five'. The B-17G currently owned by the Grissom Museum is painted in tribute to Miss Liberty Belle and is a further memorial to those who lost their lives on that August day in 1944.

BRAVERY OVER POTTON

The morning of 19th of October 1944 saw Tempsford airfield closed in by fog. A young New Zealander, F/Lt Ross Levy, was scheduled to perform an air test in Stirling LK207 'MA-W', an aircraft that belonged to a crew who were on leave. Once the fog had cleared Levy collected the rest of the crew except for the navigator and mid-upper gunner, who were not an essential part of the test flight. The aircraft, new from the factory, left the ground at 10.59 hours and quickly began its air test manoeuvres.

Just ten minutes later the massive Stirling was making its return approach to the airfield when, according to an eye-witness, there was a sudden change in its engine noise. Looking towards the ridge the aircraft was seen to be about 2,000 feet below the cloud when, suddenly, the entire tail section, including the rear turret, fell away and came crashing down into a field near the village of Potton, carrying Sgt Patrick Kelly to his death.

Ross Levy, now fully aware that disaster was inevitable, remained at the controls of the stricken bomber as it hurtled earthward, straight towards the

19th October 1944

LOCATION
Potton, Bedfordshire

TYPE
Stirling IV

SERIAL No.
LK207 MA-W

UNIT
161 Squadron, Royal Air Force

PILOT
Flight Lieutenant Ross Victor LEVY RNZAF aged 21 - killed

CREW
Pilot Officer Wilfred George ATKINSON (Flight Engineer) - aged 24 - killed

Flying Officer James William STIGGER (Air Bomber) - aged 21 - killed

Flight Sergeant Albert James COVENEY (W/Op/Air Gunner) - aged 21 - killed

Sergeant Patrick KELLY (Air Gunner) - aged 21 - killed

little school in Potton where over 300 children were enjoying a mid-morning break. It is more than likely that all control was lost but somehow, with all his strength, F/Lt Levy managed to steer the fuselage away from the playground and avoided a terrible disaster. His selfless action cost him his life, and that of his crewmates, but saved very many on the ground. An examination of the wreckage later revealed that it had suffered structural failure of the rear fuselage just forward of the tail-plane.

In the weeks that followed the crash the local schoolmaster wrote to F/Lt Levy's mother saying, "You've no idea what we thought when we saw the plane heading for the school, with 300 children. Your son managed to hedgehop the plane away from the school." Another letter from the local vicar expressed, "gratitude for the cool courage and strenuous effort and great skill of the pilot who steered the fast-disintegrating plane over the school into a field beyond, and so protected them from harm and death." As a result of Ross Levy's action, the village collected £100 for the RNZAF Benevolent Fund, and held a special ceremony where a mounted a photograph of him was given a permanent place of honour.

Above: Flt Lt Ross Victor Levy RNZAF

F/Lt Levy is buried at Cambridge City Cemetery. P/O Atkinson is buried at Gorton Cemetery, Manchester. F/Sgt Coveney is buried at Sutton Cemetery. Sgt Kelly is buried at Tottenham Cemetery and F/O Stigger is buried at Willesden New Cemetery.

The Crash Site Today

Although difficult to locate, the precise crash site can still be found today. The original crash photos provide the reader with a good perspective on where the tail section landed.

Above: The tail section of Stirling LK207 which broke off on the approach to Tempsford causing the inevitable crash. These views show the forward part of the tail section looking aft towards the rear turret fairing.

DEATH RAINS DOWN ON THURLEIGH

The men of the 305th Bomb Group had been woken early on 22nd October 1944. The aircrews filled the briefing rooms and there was anticipation in the air as they waited to hear where their target was to be that day. On this occasion it was Germany, a tank factory to the north-west of Hannover to be precise. As the crews made their way to their waiting aircraft there was the usual sense of tension as each man wondered if he would make it back safely to the ground this time. For some, like 2nd Lieutenant John Mitchell of the 364th Squadron, there would be new experiences too. Having recently arrived in England he had flown as co-pilot on several missions with other, more experienced, crews but had only flown his own aircraft on a couple of occasions.

After leaving the safety of Chelveston airfield the squadrons of the 305th Bomb Group took their place in the formation and made their way towards the target. The weather had been fair and the overall mission went well. However, upon their return, the weather had closed in over southern England and the cloud base had reduced to just a few thousand feet. Visibility was poor as the aircraft of the 305th began arriving at Chelveston and home, but there was a problem. It appears that one of the aircraft burst a tyre as it landed and blocked the runway. This now forced the aircraft following behind to continue to circle the airfield whilst the damaged B-17 was removed. A serious situation was developing as the waiting aircraft flew around in the murky overcast, passing over Thurleigh as they did so. It was at this point that some of the pilots of the 364th Squadron became aware of dim shapes ahead. These were the B-17s of the 422nd Squadron and they appeared to be heading right for the 364th, and inevitable disaster.

22nd October 1944

LOCATION
Thurleigh Airfield

TYPE
B-17G 'Flying Fortress'

SERIAL No(s)
43-38030 WF-F & 43-38133 JJ-E 'My Achin' B'

UNIT
364th & 422nd Bomb Squadrons. 305th Bomber Group (Heavy), 8th USAAF

Crew of 43-38030 WF-F 422nd Bomb Squadron	Crew of 43-38133 JJ-E 'My Achin' B' 364th Bomb Squadron
PILOT 1st Lieutenant Phil Arthur LICHTY aged 24 - killed	**PILOT** 2nd Lieutenant John MITCHELL - killed
CO PILOT 2nd Lieutenant Robert COVERSTONE aged 21 - killed	**CO PILOT** 2nd Lieutenant William C SHOEMAKER - killed
NAVIGATOR 2nd Lieutenant John L TOUCHETTE aged 28 - killed	**NAVIGATOR** 2nd Lieutenant Frank WATKINS, Jr - killed
BOMBARDIER 2nd Lieutenant Michael J VERAA - killed	**BOMBARDIER** Sergeant Phillip R MIFSUD aged 19 - killed
RADIO OPERATOR Staff Sergeant Harold E BOLING - killed	**RADIO OPERATOR** Sergeant Ashton W HEWITT - killed
FLIGHT ENGINEER Staff Sergeant Albert B ZIEGLMEIER - killed	**FLIGHT ENGINEER** Sergeant Billy F KRUG aged 20 - killed
WAIST GUNNER Staff Sergeant Ersel E LENNIER aged 20 - killed	**WAIST GUNNER** Sergeant Burton G JENKINS - killed
BALL TURRET GUNNER Staff Sergeant Nick COLAIUTA aged 24 - killed	**BALL TURRET GUNNER** Sergeant Eldon D PEACOCK - killed
TAIL GUNNER Staff Sergeant William R ROBINSON - killed	**TAIL GUNNER** Sergeant Lennard B LINSEY - killed

Above: The horrific collision caught on camera. The poor visibility as the B-17s descend through cloud is very apparent.

The Collision

The aircraft which caused the impact was that of Lt John Mitchell of the 364th Squadron. His aircraft, 43-38133 WF-E, was seen to try to avoid a collision by turning away in a steep banking manoeuvre. However, this came too late and an oncoming B-17, 43-38030 JJ-E, nicknamed 'My Achin' B', flown by 1/Lt Phil Lichty, was seen to clip the left wing of Mitchell's aircraft, slicing a large section completely off. The severed wing tip and other large pieces of debris began to fall through the air, causing chaos throughout the remaining formation. The remaining aircraft began to desperately scatter to avoid the two B-17s as they continued to break up over Thurleigh. Amazingly, a photographer on the ground managed to snap the aircraft as they collided. Debris and bodies began to rain down on Thurleigh airfield as both planes were seen to drop to the ground.

Drama on the Ground and The Aftermath

As the two B-17s fell from the sky the dramatic scenes were captured by a photographer of the 306th Bomb Group. Stunned airmen are seen in the

Bedfordshire [119]

dispersal areas and on the airfield where the burning wreckage of the two aircraft lay strewn around. One photo also shows the bodies of some of the aircrew as they lay where they fell, so close to home and the safety of Chelveston. It is hard to imagine how helpless these men felt when they saw their comrades' lifeless bodies strewn across Thurleigh airfield. Aircrew faced death and danger on every sortie but it was not often that ground personnel came face to face with death in this manner, and it must have been a great shock for them.

2/Lt Robert Coverstone

Robert Coverstone was born on 14th July 1923 in Grants Pass, Josephine, Oregon, USA the son of Virgil and Ethel Velma Coverstone. The family later moved to California, from where Robert joined the U.S. Army Air Corps. Following the death of his son, Virgil Coverstone, understandably, wanted to know how Robert had died. On 4th November 1944 both the Squadron Commander and the Chaplain wrote to Virgil Coverstone but, due to changes in the U.S. Army security policy, the letters were returned to VIII Bomber Command. Subsequently, as he had not heard any news regarding the loss of his son, Virgil wrote an impassioned letter to General 'Hap' Arnold pleading for the details of what had happened. Eventually, in January 1945, Virgil was notified of the circumstances of the accident. Robert Coverstone is buried in Plot F Row 7 Grave 37 of the American Military Cemetery, Cambridge. He was awarded an Air Medal with 2 Oak Leaf Clusters.

This page and opposite:
The scene at Thurleigh immediately after the collision with bodies and wreckage strewn far and wide.

The Crash Site Today and the Ghosts of Thurleigh

Thurlcigh continues to be an active and thriving site, although aircraft no longer fly from the airfield. With the end of military control, the site was divided into two parts. The southern part is now known as Thurleigh Business Park, and includes the runway, which is currently used for the mass storage of new cars, although it remains intact for possible future use. The northern part houses the Bedford Autodrome, as well as 306th Bomb Group Museum which is dedicated primarily to the airfield and life in the area during World War 2. It is said, by some, that the ghosts of aircrew exist at Thurleigh. One man reported smelling breakfast being cooked, even though he was in the middle of an empty car park. He was later told that the location where he stood was once the site of mess tents. Other places on the airfield are also said to have their own ghosts. The Officer's Mess is said to be home to ghostly footsteps, while policemen patrolling the airfield, apparently, peered into an empty hut on one occasion, only to see a group of airmen playing cards. If you make a visit to Thurleigh today, and you listen carefully, you may just hear the distant sound of B-17s as they pass through the overcast, still heading for home.

Burial and Personal Details

The bodies of the two crews were originally buried together in the American Cemetery in Cambridge. The post-war policy of repatriation meant that the bodies of many airmen were returned to their home towns or national cemeteries, such as Arlington, for final burial and, as a result, crews were split up. Although the bodies of 1/Lt Phil Lichty, 2/Lt John Touchett and S/Sgt William Robinson were returned to the U.S. the rest of the crew of 43-38030 remain in Cambridge. It is, however, a different matter when looking at the crew of 'My Achin' B". It has not been possible to locate the whereabouts of many of the crew of this aircraft with the exception of the flight engineer and radio operator. The only member of the crew to remain in Cambridge is Sgt Philip Mifsud. If the reader knows the grave location of the remaining members of 43-38133, the author would be most interested to hear from you.

Bedfordshire

1945

AN EAGLE LANDS IN BIGGLESWADE

2/Lt Vance C. Harney began operations with 356th Fighter Group in November 1944 and had completed 21 combat missions at the time of his death. Official reports show that he took off from Martlesham Heath at 09.31 hours on 16th January 1945, as part of an operational escort mission accompanying bombers on a raid deep into Germany. Shortly after crossing the Zuider Zee near Egmond his P-51 Mustang fighter began to suffer with engine problems and 2/Lt Harney motioned to his flight commander, Captain Bruner, that he was returning to base. He indicated, by using sign language, that he did not need an escort.

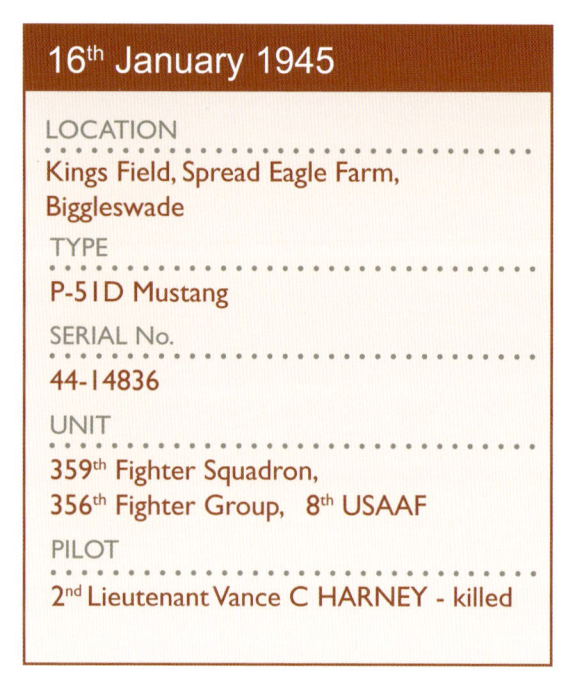

16th January 1945

LOCATION
Kings Field, Spread Eagle Farm, Biggleswade

TYPE
P-51D Mustang

SERIAL No.
44-14836

UNIT
359th Fighter Squadron, 356th Fighter Group, 8th USAAF

PILOT
2nd Lieutenant Vance C HARNEY - killed

It is believed his radio was not working and, as a result, could not be warned of changing weather conditions in England nor could he communicate with his base. As he flew across East Anglia it seems that he was trying to establish his position by getting below the low cloud cover. However, the engine problem had, by then, grown much more serious and he may have been contemplating a crash landing. A few months earlier, on 12th November 1944, Harney had survived a crash at Stansted when his P-47D Thunderbolt (42-26309) was involved in a landing accident. The thoughts of what his commanding officer and his colleagues would have said to another accident may well have been uppermost in his thoughts as he sped over the English countryside.

Above:
2/Lt Vance Harney

The stricken aircraft was seen in its last moments by two eyewitnesses. The first, 35 year-old Arthur Robinson of Potton Road, Biggleswade, said in a statement to Captain Walter Baumgarten of the U.S. Medical Corps that at about 1.50 p.m. he was picking Brussels sprouts in Kings Field, Eagle Farm, when he heard a roaring noise and on looking up saw a fighter aircraft break through the low cloud cover. It was roaring down at a terrific speed, and a slight trail of smoke could be seen. Just before hitting the ground it made a right angle turn and had burst into flames on crashing. The other witness, 50 year old Jacob Pope of Drove Road, Biggleswade, told Captain Baumgarten that at about 1.50 p.m. he was riding his bicycle along Drove Road when he saw a fighter aircraft, which was at a height of about 200 - 300 feet, cross over the road proceeding in an easterly direction. The aircraft was making a much noisier sound than usual and from the rear part of the plane a bright red glow, appearing about a foot long, was visible.

He stated that the aircraft was travelling very fast and in a straight line and that the engine noise was like a very harsh buzzing. When he had travelled a further 30 yards he saw the plane had crashed in flames. The weather was very hazy and patchy, the plane appearing and disappearing in its flight.

A variety of emergency services attended the scene including the NFS, police and an RAF fire tender. It was soon established that the pilot had been killed and his body was extracted. 2/Lt Harney was taken to the mortuary at RAF Tempsford. He was initially buried in the U.S. Cemetery in Cambridge but in December 1948 his body was exhumed and returned to the USA where it was re-interred in Park County, Indiana.

On 25th January 1945 an Accident Review Board led by Lt Col William J. Kennedy, Major James N. Wood and Major Richard A Rann determined that there were insufficient facts available to establish the specific cause of the accident. All that was known is that while the group was on the mission the bases over England became closed in due to adverse weather conditions and the remainder of the group was notified to land on the continent, which they did without further incident.

The Crash Site Today

Spread Eagle Farm was demolished in 1960 and the precise location of the crash site lies at an undefined point along Eagle Farm Road. The area has been significantly developed during the time that has elapsed and it is highly probable that the crash site has since been built upon.

(Sources: *USAAF MACR. US National Archives. Biggleswade Historical Society*)

A VALENTINE'S DAY DISASTER OVER SANDY

On February 14th 1945 a P-51B Mustang fighter of 383rd Fighter Squadron, 364th Fighter Group, piloted by Flight Officer Thomas W. Kiley took off from RAF Honington to undertake a training flight. The aircraft had previously been operating with the 355th Fighter Group where it was the mount of several Ace fighter pilots, including Captain Henry W. 'Baby' Brown who had named it 'The Hun Hunter~Texas'. It had seen a great deal of action and had been responsible for the destruction of 15 enemy aircraft, including a Ju87 Stuka shot down over Normandy on 6th June 1944. It must have conjured up many thoughts for the young trainee pilot as he tore across the darkened skies over Anglia in one of the highest scoring single aircraft of the USAAF.

Above:
The Hun Hunter - Texas had been the mount of several ace pilots of the Eighth Air Force.

Kiley, who had joined the USAAF on 23rd February 1943, was making an unauthorised pass over RAF Tempsford when he spotted a lone bomber in the overcast skies and swooped down to carry out a 'mock' attack on the aircraft, Short Stirling LK236 of 161 Squadron, piloted by Flying Officer Timperley, which was returning to Tempsford from an exercise flight. The fighter bore down on the unsuspecting bomber at very high speed and abruptly collided with the Stirling, striking the fuselage between the wings and the tail and causing the aircraft to be cut in two. The main fuselage fell on one side of Potton Lane to the east of Sandy, very near to where the Sandy Heath transmitter now stands, and the tail section on the other side of the lane. The Mustang crashed near Cambridge Road, Sandy, in the vicinity of the railway station. Thomas Kiley, of Essex County, New Jersey and all the aircrew of the Stirling were tragically killed. An accident investigation found that F/O Kiley had misjudged the distance between the two aircraft in conditions of poor visibility and was totally responsible for the collision.

14th February 1945

	LOCATION
	Sandy
TYPE	**TYPE**
P-51D	Short Stirling
SERIAL No.	**SERIAL NUMBER**
42-106448	LK236 MA-Y
UNIT	**UNIT**
383rd Fighter Squadron, 364th Fighter Group, 8th USAAF	161 (Special Duties) Squadron, Royal Air Force
PILOT	**PILOT**
Flight Officer Thomas W KILEY aged 20 - killed	Flying Officer Eric TIMPERLEY aged 24 - killed
	FLIGHT ENGINEER
	Sergeant Derek Howard MAYERS aged 19 - killed
	NAVIGATOR
	Flight Sergeant Peter Norman CARR aged 21 - killed
	RADIO OPERATOR
	Flying Officer George Colin WIGGINS (RAAF) aged 28 - killed
	AIR GUNNER
	Flight Sergeant Cyril William SAUNDERS (RAAF) aged 25 - killed
	AIR GUNNER
	Sergeant Peter Norman ELLIS aged 20 - killed
	AIR GUNNER
	Sergeant William George CORNISH aged 31 - killed

Above: F/Sgt Peter Norman Carr.

F/O Timperley is remembered at Stockport Crematorium. F/Sgt Carr, Sgt Ellis, F/Sgt Saunders and F/O Wiggins are buried at Cambridge City Cemetery. Sgt Cornish is buried at the Woodburn Cemetery, Buckinghamshire. Sgt Mayers is buried at Stockport (Willow Grove) Cemetery. Flight Officer Thomas W. Kiley is buried in the American Military Cemetery, Cambridge. In the National

Opposite page top:
Flying Officer Eric Timperley and his crew with their Stirling shortly before they died.

Opposite page bottom:
The funeral of some of the crew took place in Cambridge City cemetery.

Archives you can find the original Operations Record Book for 161 Squadron and within its contents are the photographs of the funeral for those men who were buried in Cambridge City Cemetery.

The Crash Site Today

In October 1991 the crash site of the Stirling was visited by Jack Swayn and his son, Lex, along with members of the Potton Historical Society. Jack is the brother-in-law of Flight Sergeant Bill Saunders and made the 12,000 mile pilgrimage from Brisbane to the location on Sandy Heath to honour the memory of an airman he described as, "a very dear relative and a wonderful man". The families of those who were lost in the accident were not given the full details regarding what had happened and in an interview with a reporter from the Biggleswade Chronicle Lex explained, "One of the reasons we were not told much was the secrecy of the operations." Today, both the Squadron ORB and the Air Accident Investigation records tell the full story of this tragic story.

(Sources: USAAF MACR. UK National Archives. US National Archives. Biggleswade Historical Society)

Left: Flying Officer George Wiggins the Stirling's radio operator.

Right: Flight Sergeant Cyril Saunders, one of the air gunners aboard.

A BELGIAN DIES AT FLITWICK

On 25th February 1945 Sergeant Jacques Bonnewit, a Belgian, and his navigator, Sergeant John Muncaster were briefed to carry out a ground controlled interception exercise in their Mosquito XVII (HK304). The two crewmen took off from RAF Cranfield at 10.50 hours into a fine, clear sky and remained in constant radio contact with the ground until the exercise had been completed at 12.28 hours. The pilot was then instructed to reduce his altitude from 10,000 to 4000ft and a few minutes later eye witnesses on the ground saw the aircraft flying over the Ampthill/Flitwick area from a south-westerly direction, which was quite normal for aircraft flying into Cranfield. As the aircraft approached Steppingley it was seen to spin and dive down to height of less than 1000ft. The Mosquito made a recovery but, as it did so, the wings and part of the tailplane broke away. The remaining centre fuselage then crashed to earth between Steppingly and Flitwick, exploding in a fireball at Woodside Field, Valley Farm, Flitwick. The pilot and navigator did not have time to escape the stricken aircraft and perished in the crash.

The body of Sergeant Bonnewit was repatriated to Belgium after the war and that of Sergeant Muncaster is buried in Maryport Cemetery, Cumberland.

24th February 1945

LOCATION
Woodside Field, Valley Farm, Flitwick

TYPE
de Havilland Mosquito XVII

SERIAL No.
HK304

UNIT
51 Operational Training Unit, Royal Air Force

PILOT
Sergeant Jacques L BONNEWIT killed

CREW
Sergeant John William MUNCASTER (Navigator) aged 20 - killed

Above: A HK serialled Mosquito night fighter similar to the one that crashed at Flitwick.

ANNIVERSARY LOSS
A P-47 AT ASTWOOD

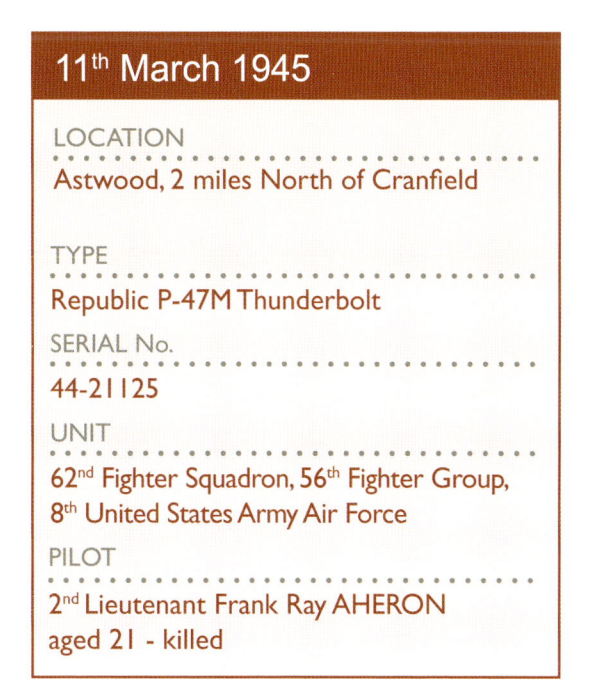

11th March 1945

LOCATION
Astwood, 2 miles North of Cranfield

TYPE
Republic P-47M Thunderbolt

SERIAL No.
44-21125

UNIT
62nd Fighter Squadron, 56th Fighter Group, 8th United States Army Air Force

PILOT
2nd Lieutenant Frank Ray AHERON aged 21 - killed

The 56th Fighter Group was one of the legendary fighter units of World War 2. It was led by the tenacious and inspiring Colonel Hubert 'Hub' Zemke and flew the rugged Republic P-47 Thunderbolt, also known as the 'Juggernaut'. The unit aggressively took the air war into the enemy heartland by employing innovative tactics, devised by Zemke, and flew bomber escort and counter-air missions across Europe. Over a period of two years its pilots destroyed more than a thousand enemy aircraft and produced 39 aces, including Francis 'Gabby' Gabreski and Robert S. Johnson.

The P-47M was a conservative attempt to come up with a higher-performance version of the Thunderbolt. Three P-47Ds were modified into prototype YP-47Ms by fitting the R-2800-57(C) engine and the GE CH-5 turbo-supercharger. The YP-47M had a top speed of 410 knots (473 mph, 761 km/h) and it was put into limited production with 130 built. However, the type suffered serious teething problems in the field due to the highly-tuned engine, and by the time the bugs were worked out, the war in Europe was over.

Amongst the pilots of the 62nd Fighter Squadron was Frank Aheron who was born in Leaksville, Rockingham, North Carolina on 4th September 1923. He married Eileen Theresa Matthews on 11th March 1944 in Dallas County, Alabama, just before he left for England. On 4th December 1944 the VIII Bomber Command attacked vital railway targets in Germany. The force of eleven hundred bombers was protected by nine hundred 'Little Friends' from Fighter Command, one of which was flown by 2/Lt Aheron. There was some initial confusion over where the bombers were to be met and vital fuel was wasted in achieving the

Bedfordshire [129]

right location. Coupled with this was the fact that there were very high winds that had not been reported and, as there were no enemy fighters present, targets of opportunity were sought on the ground, which included a high number of German aircraft at Neuberg airfield. The resulting fuel consumption meant that a number of fighters were unable to make it back to Boxted. Frank Aheron was one of those that did not make it back, bring his aircraft into St.Trond airfield for a belly landing. He eventually made it back to Boxted on 7th December. Then, on 14th January 1945, Frank Aheron took part in a fighter sweep to the Magdeburg area of Germany. During this sortie the squadron became heavily engaged with some Me109s and Frank claimed one as probably destroyed.

A P-47D of the 62nd FS flown by the C/O Col David Schilling before he replaced it with the P-47M that crashed at Astwood.

On 11th March 1945, his first wedding anniversary, Frank Aheron took to the air from RAF Boxted on a short training flight. He was flying Thunderbolt, 44-21125, which had originally been the mount of the squadron C.O. Colonel David C. Schilling, although he had not flown this particular aircraft operationally. During the training flight the Thunderbolt suffered a piston failure and this caused the oil tank to rupture. Oil now began to gush from the damaged tank, covering the windshield in a thick black coating. Frank Aheron, unable to see, decided to bring the aircraft into Cranfield for an emergency landing. It is uncertain if he stalled the aircraft or misjudged his approach, but the fighter crashed to earth at Astwood near Cranfield, killing the pilot instantly.

His body was originally buried in the American Military Cemetery in Cambridge but was repatriated after the war and on 13th August 1948 was finally laid to rest in the Raleigh National Cemetery, North Carolina.

AND STILL THEY FELL ACCIDENTS POST WW2

Despite the fact that the war in Europe had drawn to a successful close the number of fatal aviation accidents throughout the UK and the Continent continued, especially now that the RAF was turning its vast resources to the transporting of former Allied prisoners of war back to the UK. There were a number of accidents that resulted in high fatalities, simply due to the fact that aircraft were overloaded with men and women eager to escape the harsh realities of prison camp life and return to their loved ones. The war in the Far East was still not concluded and aircrew continued to train in the UK in preparation for service is this theatre of operations. Training accidents continued throughout Bedfordshire in the months following the war's end. It is not possible to list every event, therefore, I have selected some examples where the accident ended in the tragic loss of life.

A TEMPEST STRIKES MEPPERSHALL

26th June 1945

LOCATION
Meppershall

TYPE
Hawker Tempest II

SERIAL No.
MW753

UNIT
13 Maintenance Unit

PILOT
Flying Officer Normal Frederick HEWITT aged 29 - killed

Norman Hewitt was a pilot of considerable experience with over a 1,000 flying hours under his belt. He had been awarded his wings on 19th August 1940 and had flown Spitfires and Mosquitos on many occasions, but only had limited experience in flying the Tempest. At 16.40pm on 26th June 1945 he took off from RAF Henlow to carry out a test flight in MW753 after a new aileron had been fitted. The Tempest had been built by Hawker Aircraft Ltd on 14th March 1945 and had been transferred to No.13 MU on 14th May. On its initial test flight on 21st June, and on a subsequent test the same day, it was

Bedfordshire [131]

found that the aircraft was flying with its right wing low. A check of the ailerons revealed that the starboard one was faulty and it was duly replaced. The pilot had indicated his intention to carry out a roll in the aircraft to ensure that the aileron was working properly. About 10 minutes after leaving the ground the aircraft was seen at a height of about 1,500 to 2,000 feet heading in an easterly direction. It then made a 180 degree turn and went into a shallow dive on the airfield. When it was over the centre of the airfield it was seen to carry out a normal roll to port at a height that was described by various witnesses as being between 350 to 1,500 feet.

Opinion varies over what happened next, but it would appear that the aircraft either carried out another roll or fell into a spin from which it did not recover. It struck the ground about a mile west of the airfield near the village of Meppershall, killing instantly the pilot. The aircraft, with 145 gallons of aviation fuel aboard, was severely damaged but, despite this, a fire did not break out and this provided the accident investigators with a greater opportunity to examine the wreckage. There were several witnesses to the crash but their version of events varied and this led to some doubt as to how that accident had happened. In the end the investigators determined that, given the lack of structural evidence at the crash scene, the probable cause was a loss of control by the pilot after having carried out a slow roll at far too low a height. Norman Hewitt is buried in St.Mary's Churchyard, Henlow.

The Crash Site Today

The crash site is easily located and can be viewed on Google Earth. Not much has changed since the day that Norman Hewitt's Tempest struck the ground, although I did not find any surface debris when walking along the public footpath by the side of the location. The original crash photos clearly show the impact site and can easily be aligned with the current tree line. As always, the reader should ensure that they have been granted access rights by any landowners before attempting to visit the location of this, or any other, crash site.

Opposite page: The wreckage of Tempest MW753 at Meppershall.

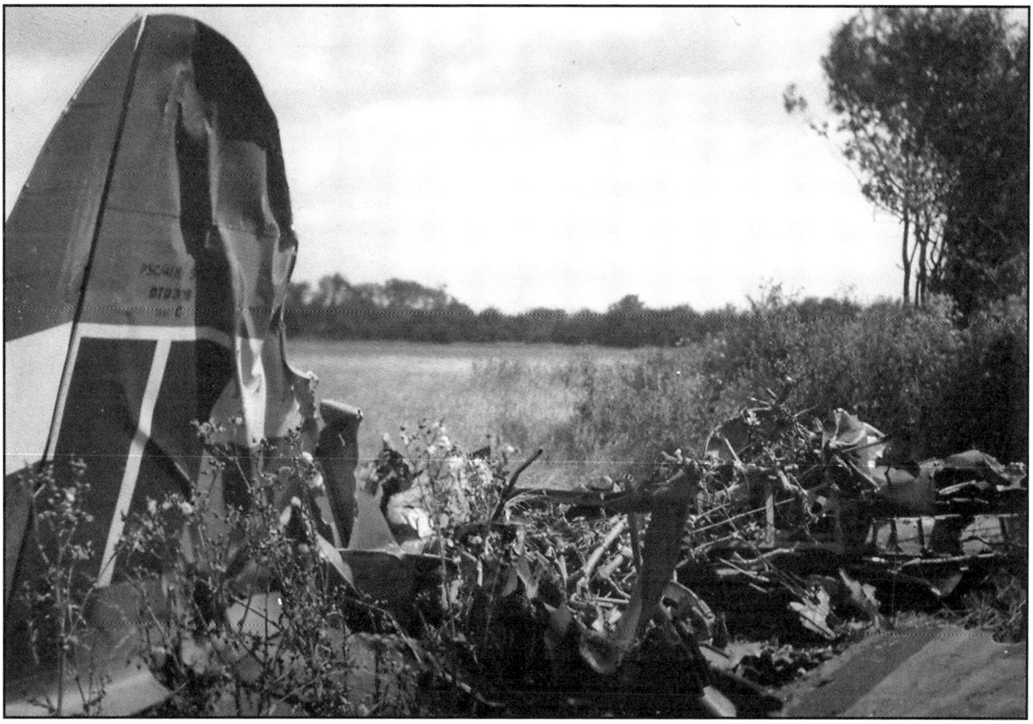

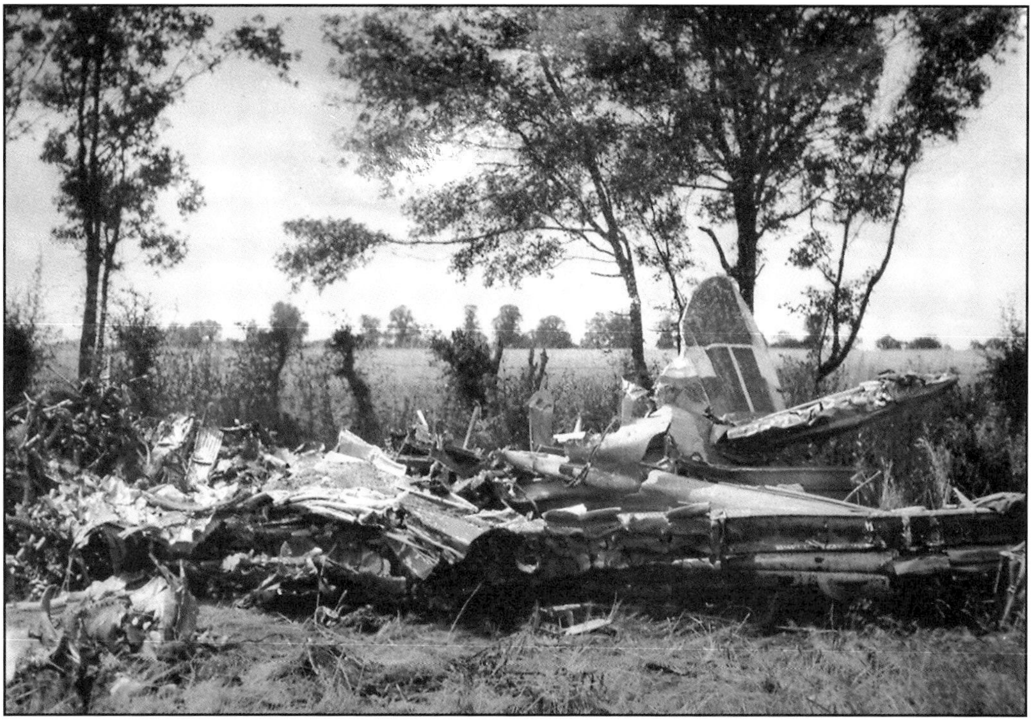

THE POTTON WOOD LIBERATOR

The Pilot and Instructor

F/Lt Patrick McNulty begun his flying career in October 1942 at Narromine, New South Wales, and continued his training in both Canada and the UK. Eventually, he undertook his conversion training to Halifax bombers between June and August 1944 and commenced operational flights with No.466 (RAAF) Squadron at Driffield from 22nd August 1944 until 13th February 1945. He was awarded the Distinguished Flying Cross on 13th July 1945 for his actions whilst serving as a Flight Sergeant with No.356 Squadron. The citation reads as follows;

"This airman has taken part in very many sorties as a flight engineer and has invariably displayed a high standard of devotion to duty. On one occasion, when attacking enemy positions on Ramree Island, his aircraft was hit by anti-aircraft fire during the bombing run. Flight Sergeant McNulty was heavily thrown and temporarily stunned. A fire started in the floor of the aircraft. Flight Sergeant McNulty, who had quickly recovered, promptly directed his energies towards quelling the flames. Disregarding the danger from bursting oxygen bottles and from exploding bullets this resolute airman subdued the flames by means of extinguishers and finally put out the remains of

18th September 1945

LOCATION
Potton Wood, Cockayne Hatley

TYPE
Consolidated Liberator GR VIII

SERIAL No.
KN736

UNIT
466 Squadron, Royal Air Force

PILOT
Flight Lieutenant Patrick Joseph McNULTY DFC (Pilot Under Instruction) aged 22 - killed

CREW
Flight Lieutenant Edward John James SPILLER DFC
(Instructor) aged 28 - killed
Warrant Officer James Raymond POTTER
(Radio Operator) aged 28 - killed
Flight Sergeant Delbert Roy TURNER
(Flight Engineer) aged 20 - killed
Flight Sergeant R V CARLING
(Instructor Flight Engineer) seriously injured
Flight Officer N P GILMOUR
(Pupil Navigator) Seriously injured
Flight Officer F G DOAK
(Pupil Pilot) Slightly Injured

the fire by smothering it with his flying suit. He displayed courage, resolution and devotion to duty of a high standard."

In September 1945 No.466 Squadron began converting to Consolidated Liberators and F/Lt McNulty was undergoing his conversion training at RAF Bassingbourne. He was being instructed by Flight Lieutenant Edward Spiller who was regarded as an above average pilot and had been in the RAF since March 1939. Spiller had a great deal of operational experience on Liberators and had served with several operational squadrons between July 1941 and September 1945. He had been attached to RAF Bassingbourn as a Liberator instructor on 17th September and this was only his second instructional flight. He had been awarded the Distinguished Flying Cross on 8th June 1943 for his actions whilst serving as a Warrant Officer with No.224 Squadron. The citation reads as follows;

"This officer has completed a very large number of hours flying on operations, and has displayed outstanding efficiency and unfailing devotion to duty. During a patrol in May, 1943, his aircraft was attacked by 10 Junkers 88s. For nearly half an hour a running fight ensued and Warrant Officer Spiller displayed great skill and courage in frustrating the attackers. Although his aircraft was damaged he flew it to base, where he effected a masterly landing without the aid of brakes or flaps. Warrant Officer Spiller set a most inspiring example."

Below: A Liberator GRVIII similar to the one that crashed at Potton Wood.

On 18th September 1945 F/Lt Spiller had been given authority to demonstrate both single and twin-engined flying performance on the massive four-engined plane. At 17.41 hours it lifted off from the tarmac at RAF Bassingbourn with seven men aboard. F/Lt Mcnulty was flying the Liberator and almost immediately after leaving the ground the instructor throttled back the starboard outer engine and feathered the propeller. The heavy aircraft continued to climb until reached a height of about 1,100 feet where F/Lt Spiller then throttled back the starboard inner engine and, again, feathered the propeller. McNulty continued to fly the aircraft on the port engines but allowed the speed to drop to about 110 knots, whereby the Liberator began to lose height. It was at this point that the instructor realised that the ground was in close proximity and attempted to bring the starboard propellers back to life. Despite his action the engines were unable to provide the power required to correct the situation and McNulty applied full port aileron in an effort to keep the starboard wing up but the drag on the wing caused the aircraft to continue to turn to starboard. Eventually, the giant Liberator could not maintain height and the starboard wing struck the ground at the edge of Potton Wood, cartwheeled and came to rest some 80 yards inside the wood, where a fire broke out.

The cause of the accident was deemed to be as a result of a combination of low air speed and two wind-milling propellers on one side. The feathering of engines below 3,000 feet was contrary to standing orders and it was believed that the ignition switches may have been in the 'off' position which would explain why the two engines would not develop power. As a secondary issue, it was found that the crew were neither wearing nor carrying parachutes.

F/Lt Edward Spiller is buried in Edmonton Cemetery, Middlesex. F/Sgt Delbert Turner is buried in Lowestoft Cemetery, Suffolk. F/Lt Patrick McNulty and W/O James Potter are buried in the Cambridge City Cemetery.

Below: The distinctive head-on profile of a B-24.

THE CRANFIELD VICTOR

14th July 1954

LOCATION
Cranfield

TYPE
Handley-Page Victor HP80 Prototype

SERIAL No.
WB771

UNIT
Royal Aircraft Establishment

PILOT
Squadron Leader Ronald Vivian ECCLESTONE DFC AFC
aged 31 - Test pilot - killed

CREW
Mr Ian Kenneth BENNETT
aged 29 - Flight Test Observer - killed
Mr Bruce HEITHERSAY
aged 28 - Flight Test Observer - killed
Mr Albert Bernard COOK
aged 24 - Flight Test Observer - killed

The Aircraft

Handley-Page Victor WB771 was the first of two HP80 prototypes. It had been built at their factory in Radlett and although there was a runway there the Government had decided that the longer runway at Boscombe Down would provide an additional margin of safety. The huge aircraft was then transported, with some difficulty, by road to the test center for flight trials. Once WB771 had been reassembled at Boscombe Down it was run through ground hydraulic tests in preparation for an initial flight. During these preparations a fire broke out and doused three technicians with burning hydraulic fluid, one of them dying in the hospital a few weeks later. The aircraft was finally ready to take to the air and performed its initial flight on 24th December 1952, with Handley-Page's chief test pilot, Squadron Leader Hedley George Hazelden, at the controls. He described the initial flight as 'comfortable' with 'no anxieties'. The takeoff run was surprisingly short and there had been no real need to move the machine to Boscombe Down. WB771 made an appearance at the Farnborough Air Show in 1953. Trials showed the basic design to be sound, with only some small corrections needed. Unfortunately, one of the corrections was discovered the hard way.

On 14th July 1954 it undertook a position error calibration flight which involved level runs at 100 feet over Cranfield, at ever increasing speeds. After numerous runs over the airfield, induced tail flutter caused cracking of the bolt holes in the fin. These allowed the three bolts securing the tailplane to loosen and shear in quick succession. The complete tailplane and elevators broke away from the aircraft. The remainder of

Bedfordshire [137]

the aircraft dived into the ground at full power, striking exactly at the intersection of the two Cranfield runways. Ronald Ecclestone and his crew were all killed instantly. It was found that the aircraft were considerably tail-heavy and this was remedied by large ballast weights in the other HP.80 prototype. The Victor was the last of the V-bombers to enter service and the last to retire. It saw service in the Falklands War and in the 1991 Gulf War as an in-flight refuelling tanker.

The Crew

The captain, Squadron Leader Ronald Vivian 'Taffy' Ecclestone DFC was from Aldershot and was a graduate of the Empire Test Pilots' School, No.8 Course in 1949. He had recently joined Handley Page as a test pilot and had accepted the task of flying the Victor so that the senior company test pilot could carry out a demonstration of another aircraft to a foreign sales delegation. During the Second World War he had flown Stirlings and Lancasters in Bomber Command and had been awarded the DFC following a tour with No.218 Squadron. He had also flown Hurricanes and Spitfires in the Bomber Defence Tactical Unit and was later engaged in development flying at Marham, Boscombe Down and Farnborough. He had served for a year in the Directorate of Operational Requirements at the Air Ministry and had joined Handley Page Ltd less than three months before the accident. The Handley Page flight test observer, Ian Bennett, came from St Albans and had been one of the two-man crew who made the first flight in a Victor in December 1952. Also killed were Handley Page flight test observers Bruce Heithersay, a former member of the Royal Australian Air Force who was living at St Albans, and Albert Bernard Cook of Edgware, London.

Below: The futuristic lines of the prototype Victor WB771 are clearly apparent in this landing view at Farnborough.

BOMBS AND ROCKETS IN BEDFORDSHIRE

Luftwaffe Air Raids

Throughout the Second World War Bedfordshire suffered numerous attacks by the Luftwaffe, due mainly to its proximity to both London and the Midlands. Although a majority of raids were carried out by large groups of aircraft, occasionally single aircraft also made lone raids, either in a desperate attempt to dump their payloads and return to their bases, or whilst making 'hit & run' sneak attacks on random targets before they encountered the fighters of the RAF. There is not provision within this publication to record every incident but I have highlighted those air raids where there was loss of life inflicted upon both civilians and servicemen alike. Civilians who died as a result of enemy action during the Second World War are commemorated differently to those who died as a result of military service. Their names are recorded on the Civilian War Dead Roll of Honour located in St George's Chapel in Westminster Abbey and their individual records can be found on the Commonwealth War Grave Commission website and in the record books held at the National Archives

RAIDERS AT VAUXHALL

In June 1940 the specifications for the new Infantry Tank Mark IV, nicknamed the Churchill, were given to the design team at the Vauxhall plant in Luton. By July of that year the design was complete and the factory began gearing up for production of the prototypes. With the site now switching to vital war work, and its close proximity to Luton airport, it became a prime target for the Luftwaffe. On Friday August 30th, 1940, Luton suffered its first, and one of its worst, air raids of World War Two. Twenty enemy aircraft dropped bombs in and around the Vauxhall plant area. Most of the bombs fell on Vauxhall Motors, Luton Airport and Caddington but seven of them hit the Church Cemetery in Crawley Green Road and three

30th August 1940

LOCATION
Luton

landed on Hayward Tyler in Windmill Road but did not explode. Several more unexploded bombs landed on fields adjoining Farley Farm. Several civilian areas were bombed, including Albert Road, Baker Street, Cambridge Street, Chequer Street, Chobham Street, Cowper Street, Cutenhoe Road, Farley Avenue, Farley Green Cottages, Harcourt Street, Langley Street, Manor Road Recreation Ground, Milton Road, Park Street, Queen Street, Russell Rise, Seymour Avenue, Strathmore Avenue, Tennyson Road, Wellington Street and Windsor Street. The Salisbury Arms Hotel at the corner of Windsor Street and Wellington Street was demolished. 59 people were killed with 60 being seriously injured and another 81 slightly wounded. A 1,000 kilo device hit the Park Street bus depot, killing one employee and injuring 12. A pall of smoke rose high above the bomb-hit Vauxhall plant but production at the factory was not badly affected, although sadly many of the paint workers were among those killed on the day.

Above: Smoke billows over Luton after the 30th August raid.

Overleaf: More views of the bomb damage in Luton.

Thomas James Harris DCM

One of those who perished at the Vauxhall Works that day was 45 year-old Thomas James Harris. During the First World War he had served with the 1st Bedfordshire Regiment and had arrived in France on 16th August 1914 with the first contingent of Britain's 'contemptible little army'. He was later awarded the Distinguished Conduct Medal for gallantry in battle whilst he was serving as a Corporal (10145) during the Battle of the Somme. The citation in the London Gazette of 22nd September 1916 reads as follows;

"For conspicuous gallantry during operations. He attacked an enemy post in a wood single-handed, and killed five of the enemy. He then fetched up supports and 11 other enemy surrendered. He was wounded."

Tom Harris was later posted to the Labour Corps as his injuries prevented him from returning to a front line Regiment.

Those who died at the Vauxhall Motor Works

Harry Archer	Aged 54	16 Leicester Road
Alfred James Attfield	Aged 21	94 Crawley Green Road
George Harry Chambers	Aged 44	39 Hockliffe Road, Leighton Buzzard
Clifford Sidney Curtiss	Aged 40	42 Stanford Road, Home Guard Member
Alfred James Dean	Aged 26	20 Lyndhurst Road
Leonard Robert Farey	Aged 30	63 St Martin's Avenue
Frederick Charles Gilbert	Aged 36	66 Wigmore Lane, Stopsley
Albert Edward Green	Aged 36	9a Bucklersbury, Hitchin, Hertfordshire
Robert Alfred Halsey	Aged 19	41 Hazelbury Crescent
John Abraham Harper	Aged 15	56 Grove Road
Thomas James Harris D.C.M	Aged 45	62 Dane Road
Alexander Aitken Harrower	Aged 26	244 Beechwood Road
Iris Olive Hough	Aged 19	176 Selbourne Road
Leslie Horace Jackson	Aged 37	806 Dunstable Road
Charles Henry King	Aged 50	51 Vandyke Road, Leighton Buzzard
Oliver John Lazell	Aged 20	61 Solway Road
Richard Stephen Mann	Aged 50	11 Farley Avenue. F.A.P Member
James Henry Nieland	Aged 55	38 Bolton Road
Dennis Malcolm Orchard	Aged 15	45 Trent Road
Frederick Arthur Porter	Aged 28	43 Richmond Hill
Thomas Geoffrey Rhodes	Aged 18	20 Claremont Road
Leonard John Stoughton	Aged 44	203 Cutenhoe Road
John Glanffrwd Thomas	Aged 16	113 Chester Avenue, Leagrave
Arthur John Thompson	Aged 33	121 Westfield Road, Harpenden, Hertfordshire
William Pitt Waddington	Aged 53	116 Runley Road
Derrick West	Aged 20	122 Stathmore Avenue
Arthur Thomas Whittaker	Aged 53	21 Oakley Road

Those injured at the Vauxhall Motor Works and died the same day at Luton and Dunstable Hospital

Everard Arnold	Aged 39	Overstone Road
Evan John Breeze	Aged 47	88 Chester Avenue
William Frederick Caley-Keech	Aged 36	37 Durham Road. A.R.P Decontamination Service
Fernley George Felton	Aged 29	38 Althorpe Street
Sidney James Hales	Aged 41	56 Cutenhoe Road
Ronald Cecil Impey	Aged 28	125 Victoria Street
John Andrew Kilby	Aged 18	64 Crawley Green Road
Archibald Henry Pitkin	Aged 49	159 Selbourne Road
Eric Percy Ward	Aged 25	43 Selbourne Road
Harry John Weedon	Aged 71	3 Chester Avenue

Those injured at the Vauxhall Motor Works and died at Luton and Dunstable Hospital on 31st August 1940

Walter Henry Cocks	Aged 26	13 Saffron Road, Biggleswade
Edward Albert Crawley	Aged 38	98 Westfield Road, Harpenden, Hertfordshire
William John Gresty	Aged 51	157 Connaught Road
John Edward Woodfine	Aged 31	56 St. Ethelbert Avenue

Those killed in Luton town

William Robert Burchmore	Aged 70	Died at 97 Harcourt Street
Elizabeth Ethel Gee	Aged 54	Died at 159 Wellington Street
Jennie Guy	Aged 61	Died at 45 Seymour Road
Sydnevy James Long	Aged 49	Died at 11a Dunstable Road
Margaret Jean Morrison	Aged 2	Died at 93 Harcourt Road. Daughter of L/Cpl Morrison, RTR
John Andrew Guthrie Skelton	Aged 3	Died at 159 Wellington Street
Sheila Elizabeth Smith	Aged 8	Died at 95 Harcourt Street
Alfred Wallis	Aged 81	Died at Recreation Grounds, Manor Road

Town residents who died from injuries at Luton and Dunstable Hospital

John Eynon Wynne Hughes	Aged 10	56 Seymour Road
Ralph Lacey	Aged 32	Wentworth, Graham Gardens
Marjorie Phyllis Williams	Aged 30	120 Cowper Street

Died at Luton Corporation Transport Depot

Henry William Miles	Aged 60	7 Gloucester Road

Those who died on 2nd September 1940

Mary Elizabeth Halfpenny	Aged 18 months	119 Cambridge Street Died at the Children's Hospital
Reginald George Bonnick	Aged 29	102 Cambridge Street Died at St. Mary's Hospital

The Thompson Family who died at 79 Farley Avenue

May Thompson	Aged 35	Wife of William Arthur Thompson
Ian William Thompson	Aged 4	Died at Children's Hospital
Barbara Gladys Thompson	Aged 10 months	Died at Farley Avenue

Servicemen who died on 30th August 1940 in Luton

Sergeant Henry W Miles	Aged 60	4th Bedfordshire Bn. Home Guard
George Edward Riggs		743719 Leading Aircraftman, Royal Air Force

THE LONE RAIDERS

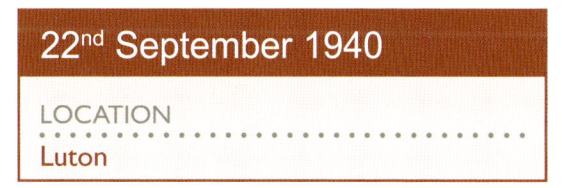

22nd September 1940

LOCATION
Luton

Just three weeks after the devastating attack on the Vauxhall plant a lone raider, probably looking to attack the plant again, dropped bombs in Park Street, Luton. Those who were killed or died of their injuries are listed below. Particularly poignant is the death of Frances Waller, who was aged just 20 months.

Charles Albert Crew	Aged 38	Died at 155 Park Street
Gladys Edna Crew	Aged 38	Wife of Charles Albert Crew Died at 155 Park Street
Louisa Emily Crew	Aged 69	Died at 155 Park Street
Mabel Crew	Aged 48	Died at 149 Park Street
Reuben Crew	Aged 48	Died at 149 Park Street
Julia Fisher	Aged 78	Died at 157 Park Street
Arthur Hartup	Aged 54	Died at 157 Park Street
Florence Emily Hartup	Aged 50	Wife of Arthur Hartup Died at 157 Park Street
Frances Mary Waller	Aged 20 months	Injured at 159 Park Street and died on 11th January 1941
Sapper Norman John Baker	Aged 19	Royal Engineers . Luton Church Burial Ground

26nd September 1940

LOCATION
RAF Henlow, Bedfordshire

At 15.55 hours on 26th September 1940 a lone twin-engined German bomber emerged from cloud some 3,000 feet above RAF Henlow. As it flew towards the airfield the ground defences began to fire at it, but with no apparent effect. It then dropped a stick of eight high explosive bombs from a north-eastern direction, one of which exploded on the tarmac of Shed 189. A second stick of bombs dropped a short distance outside the airfield boundary and demolished two houses and caused minor injuries to some civilians. Additionally, three airmen and two civilian employees were slightly injured, but not detained in hospital. The attack left Hanger 188 with damage to its roof, doors, windows and lighting as well as severe damage to two aircraft, Whitley (K7250) and Hind (K5546). Slight damage was caused to several other aircraft.

The Station Casualties for 26th September

903969 AC1 Harold Parrington	13 Maintenance Unit	Died of injuries aged 20
572493 LAC Ronald Jack Munday	13 Maintenance Unit	Died of injuries aged 18
159142 LAC Herbert Heaton	13 Maintenance Unit	Died of injuries aged 39
648341 AC1 Walter Leslie Carver	13 Maintenance Unit	Died of injuries aged 22 on 27th September 1940
550877 CPL Basil James Johnson	13 Maintenance Unit	Died of injuries aged 21 on 2nd October 1940
572206 LAC L J Eaton	13 Maintenance Unit	Died of injuries aged 21 on 2nd October 1940
25296 LAC E M Mills	13 Maintenance Unit	Injured
292127 AC2 E F Tracey	13 School of TT	Injured

On 15th October 1940 a lone German raider dropped a stick of bombs in the Old Bedford Road area of Luton, striking two hat factories. Thirteen people, mostly women and girls, were killed and another 35 injured.

15th October 1940

LOCATION
Bedford

Gladys Ansell	Aged 27	Died at 58 Old Bedford Road
Eliza Wood Borland	Aged 32	Died at 60 Old Bedford Road W.V.S Member
Stanley George Bushby	Aged 56	Died at 60 Old Bedford Road
Harry George Carter	Aged 57	Died at 60 Old Bedford Road
Gladys Winifred Chamberlain	Aged 22	Injured at Old Bedford Road and died on her way to hospital
Marian Alice Chamberlain	Aged 26	Died at 60 Old Bedford Road
Amelia Chesham	Aged 63	Injured at Old Bedford Road and died on her way to hospital
Gertrude Emily Gidding	Aged 50	Died at 60 Old Bedford Road
Harry Goode Gregory	Aged 56	Died at 58 Old Bedford Road
Joyce May Keen	Aged 15	Died at 60 Old Bedford Road
James Ross	Aged 58	Died at Old Bedford Road
Barbara May Scales	Aged 20	Died at 60 Old Bedford Road
Irene Constance Weddell	Aged 26	Died at 60 Old Bedford Road

30th June 1942

LOCATION
Bedford

On 30th June 1942 a German raider dropped two 250kg high explosive bombs on allotments near Broad Avenue causing damage to properties in the area as well as Willow Road and London Road. A large number of incendiaries were dropped around Russell Park causing four casualties, one serious, and Mile Road Isolation Hospital was damaged. One of the injured civilians, Mary Kathleen Bergen, aged 40, of 60 Broad Avenue suffered from the effects of her wounds for seven months and finally succumbed to them on 31st January 1943 when she died in the home where she had been grievously injured.

30th July 1942

LOCATION
Bedford

A heavy air raid took place on the town leaving nine people dead and sixty-one injured. Three houses were partially demolished and another thirty were rendered uninhabitable, with a further 100 houses being left with minor damage. High explosive and incendiary bombs had been dropped in Barkers Lane; Castle Road; Denby Street; Foster Street; George Street; Goldington Road; Harpur Street; Irwin Street; Kimbolton Road; Newnham Avenue; Pembroke Street; Philpotts Avenue; Putnoe Lane; Risborough Road; Russell Park; St.Albans Road; Tavistock Place and Wendover Drive. Bombs also fell on Cardington, Renhold and Salph End.

Civilian casualty list for 30th July 1942

Percy William Bandey	Aged 53	Died at The Oaks, Kimbolton Road. (Fire Watcher)
Derek Raymond Betts	Aged 8	Died at Derby Street Shelter
Judith Sheila Gridley	Aged 4	Died at 2 Putnoe Lane
Michael Anthony Gridley	Aged 7	Died at 2 Putnoe Lane
Edward William Henry Laxton	Aged 48	Died at The Oaks, Kimbolton Road
Arthur Odell	Aged 80	Injured at 32 Albert Street and died the same day at County Hospital
Pauline Barbara Roach	Aged 12	Injured at 11 Cobden Street and died at 3 Kimbolton Road
Gillian Lesley Simms	Aged 2	Injured at 28 Albert Street and died at County Hospital
Beatrice May Williamson	Aged 40	Died at 20 Pembrooke Street

THE VENGEANCE WEAPONS

The German V-weapons, short for Vergeltungswaffen (retaliation weapon), comprised of the V-1 flying bomb, the V-2 rocket and the V-3 cannon. All of these weapons were intended for use in a military campaign against Britain, though, in the event, only the V-1 and V-2 were ever used. The V-weapon offensive began on 13th June 1944 and did not come to an end until 29th March 1945. In terms of casualties, their effects had been less than their inventors had hoped, or their victims feared. Property damage was extensive with over 20,000 houses a day being damaged at the height of the campaign, causing a massive housing crisis in south-east England in late 1944 and early 1945.

The V-1

The Fieseler Fi 103, better known as the V-1, was an early pulse-jet-powered missile. Designed by Lusser and Gosslau, it had a fuselage constructed mainly of welded sheet steel and wings built of plywood. The simple pulse jet engine pulsed fifty times per second and the characteristic buzzing sound gave rise to the nicknames 'buzz bomb' or 'doodlebug'. The launch sites for the V-1 were constructed in Northern France, along the coast from Calais to Le Havre. Aerial bombing attacks on these sites by the Allied air forces were only partially successful and by June 1944 they were ready for action. Following the D-Day landings in Normandy the Germans opted to launch an assault on Britain and, early on the morning of 13th June 1944, the first V-1 flying bomb attack was carried out on London. A total of 9,251 V-1s were fired at Britain with the vast majority being aimed at London. A number fell in Bedfordshire and the following is an extract from the incident lists held by the county archives.

Opposite page: A Fieseler Fi103 V-1 or 'doodlebug' as it was more commonly known to those on the receiving end of it.

21st June 1944
LOCATION
Luton

10th December 1944
LOCATION
Henlow

24th March 1945
LOCATION
Chicksands

The first recorded V-1 flying bomb to strike Bedfordshire exploded in area of Ashcroft Road and Luton Airport on 21st June 1944. There were no known casualties.

On Sunday 10th December 1944 at approximately 19.00 hours, a V-1 approached RAF Henlow from a north-easterly direction, flying at approximately 50 to 70 feet above the ground. It crashed with the engine still running into a ploughed field 80 yards from the southern perimeter of the camp between Old Runwick Farm and railway line, causing blast damage to the Officers' Mess, WAAF Officers' Mess and two Officers' Married Quarters. There was also damage to Pollards Cottages and the Birch Brothers bus depot. Two slight casualties were reported with the wife of F/Lt F G Harley having a tooth knocked out as a result of the explosion.

On 24th March 1945 the last known V-1 flying bomb to be launched against Britain landed in Chicksands, Bedfordshire. There were no known casualties.

WHISPERING DEATH
A V-2 STRIKES WITHOUT WARNING

The V-2

The V-2 rocket, designed by Wernher Magnus Maximilian von Braun, was first conceived in early 1936 and was the world's earliest ballistic missile. In October 1942 the first fully operational model was launched from Peenemunde, Germany and reached an altitude of sixty miles, becoming the first rocket to reach the fringes of space. During 1943/44 the Germans built secret launching sites in Northern France but these were quickly overrun by the Allies following the D-Day invasions. Alternative launching sites were set up around The Hague in Holland and the first offensive rocket was launched from here against London on 8th September 1944. It took an estimated five minutes to fly the 200 miles to London where it smashed to earth in Chiswick, causing thirteen casualties. By October 1944 the offensive had become sustained and intercepting the supersonic missiles in flight proved impossible. Other counter measures, such as bombing the launch sites, were also fairly ineffectual. Sustained bombardment by the V-2s continued until 27th March 1945 when one of the last V-2 missiles to be launched hit a block of flats in Stepney, killing 134 people and injuring 49. 1,115 V-2s were fired at the United Kingdom killing an estimated 2,754 civilians and a further 2,917 service personnel. A handful of these fell in Bedfordshire, with the heaviest loss of life occurring in Luton on 6th November 1944. The following is an extract from the incident lists held by both the county and national archives.

6th November 1944

LOCATION
Luton

In the autumn of 1944 Luton was a hive of military activity as a multitude of industries produced goods for the Allied war machine. The Vauxhall plant was manufacturing Churchill tanks as well as the successful Bedford QL 4x4 lorry, whilst Electrolux and Skefco produced other much needed goods, such as ball bearings. It seemed that every hat factory in the town was turning out military uniforms and at the Commer-Karrier plant in Biscot Road, they were busy producing trucks for the Army. Although it was apparent to everyone that a victory was looming throughout Europe, the residents of the town were unable to avoid the ravages of the latest version of the new Nazi terror weapons, the V-2.

At eight minutes to ten on the morning of 6th November 1944 the workforce at the Commer plant saw the building of a new canteen and offices coming to an end. At that precise moment a V-2 rocket, which a few minutes before had been launched from a mobile carrier in The Hague area of Holland, struck the corner of the works and completely destroyed it, killing 19 people and injuring another 196. Some of those killed were found still standing in the place where they had taken their last breath, as the force of the blast sucked the very life out of them. One witness described how she had been waiting for the canteen wagon to come round with sandwiches when she suddenly found herself up to her neck in bricks and mortar. Only then did she hear the terrifying sound of the exploding rocket. People were running everywhere and the number of casualties was described as dreadful. Rescuers were quickly on the scene but there was a shortage of ambulances and some of the injured found themselves being taken to the Luton and Dunstable hospital in a brewery van. Although some employees at the plant were killed and injured it appears that a majority of the casualties were the residents of Biscot Road itself as many of the houses were flattened.

Up until this date the existence of the V-2 had been officially denied by the Government, but on 10th November Winston Churchill informed the House of Commons that these weapons were fact and not fiction. For the employees of Commer-Karrier, and the residents of Biscot Road, that confirmation had already been a terrifying reality.

Casualty List for 6th November 1944

Rachel Ann Baynham	Aged 62	Died at 83 Biscot Road
Beryl Carter	Aged 19 months	Died at 77 Biscot Road. Daughter of 2nd Lieut. Stanley Carter
Oscar Franklin Cross	Aged 58	50 Brampton Road, St. Albans, Hertfordshire. Died at Biscot Road
Rex Brian Glenister	Aged 17	Died at Biscot Road
George Stanley Handcock	Aged 64	Died at Biscot Road. National Fire Service Member
Elizabeth Jones	Aged 82	79 Biscot Road. Died at 81-83 Biscot Road
Norman James Moore	Aged 29	Died at 81 Biscot Road
Carole Rosemary Mortlock	Aged 20 months	Died at 81 Biscot Road
Elsie May Raines	Aged 49	Died at 58 Biscot Road
Amy Rees	Aged 43	Died at 81 Biscot Road
Cyril Jack Rixon	Aged 46	Died at 83 Biscot Road
Frank Rudd	Aged 71	Injured at 31 Biscot Road. Died the same day in hospital
Lizzie Simpkins	Aged 74	91 Althorp Road. Died at Biscot Road
Albert Henry Squires	Aged 59	20 Newbury Lane, Silsoe. Died at Commer Car Works, Biscot Road
Annie Elizabeth Thompson	Aged 69	Died at 77 Biscot Road
Peter John Wise	Aged 16 months	Died at 31 Biscot Road. Son of F/Sgt Eric Francis Wise, RAF
Sarah Rickard	Aged 65	Injured at 70 Biscot Road. Died in hospital on 18th November 1944
Isabel Blanche Mary Armitage	Aged 58	Died in Hospital on 20th November 1944

7th December 1944
LOCATION
Hayes End, Bedfordshire

10th January 1945
LOCATION
Arlesey, Bedfordshire

23rd March 1945
LOCATION
Studham, Bedfordshire

6th September 1947
LOCATION
Leighton Buzzard

At 8.08pm there was a great explosion at Hayes End as a V-2 rocket crashed into the local recreation ground. It devastated some bungalows and a man was killed in this explosion.

A V-2, launched from The Hague, exploded at City Field Farm damaging shop windows in Arlesey and left a Crater 43'x17'.

Launched by Battery 1./485 at 06.42 hours on 23rd March 1945. Seven minutes later it exploded in a field at Dagnall Hill. There were no known casualties.

52 year-old William Frederick Morris, (War Reserve Police Constable) died at 67 Hockliffe Road, Leighton Buzzard as the result of injuries received while on duty in an air raid. He is the last known civilian casualty from Bedfordshire to lose his life as a result of enemy action.

Below: The V-2 rocket, a truly terrifying weapon that would explode before the victims could even hear it coming.

BEDFORDSHIRE INCIDENT & ACCIDENT LOG

This list covers both the aircraft accidents and air raid incidents that occurred throughout Bedfordshire which resulted in a loss of life or injury. It is not exhaustive.

Date	Location	Incident
1920		
16 August	Biddenham, Beds.	Armstrong Whitworth FK8. G-EALW. Crashed on take-off from cornfield. Pilot killed. Passenger injured.
1921		
3 December	Henlow, Beds	Vickers FB27 Vimy. HAD. Crashed after take-off on delivery flight. Pilot injured, passenger killed.
1926		
10 March	Henlow, Beds	Vickers FB27 Vimy. F9184 & Avro 504K H5035. Collided in mid-air. 5 killed.
1927		
9 March	Henlow, Beds	Corporal Arthur East aged 26 - Killed in a parachute descent.
11 March	Henlow, Beds	Leading Aircraftman Ernest A Dobbs aged 26 - killed in a flying accident.
1928		
22 March	Clifton, Beds	Avro 504N J8581. Home Aircraft Depot. Crashed after striking telegraph pole. Pilot & passenger killed.
1 July	Clifton Lodge, Beds	Avro 504N H2534. 23 Squadron. Crashed during test flight. Pilot & passenger killed.
1929		
3 May	Henlow, Beds	Aircraftman 1st Class Richard F Mason aged 19 - killed in a flying accident.
3 December	Cranfield, Beds	Hawker Hind. 108 Squadron. Struck a tree whilst landing. Pilot killed.
1933		
5 December	Lidlington, Beds	GAL ST.4 Monospar. Aircraft struck a pylon and crashed at Thrupp End Farm. pilot Killed.
1936		
24 May	Dunstable, Beds	de Havilland Tiger Moth G-ADGO. Crashed at London Glider Club during a pleasure flight. Pilot injured. Passenger fatally injured.
1937		
12 October	Cranfield, Beds	Hawker Hind. Struck a tree and burst into flames on airfield. Pilot killed.
1938		
11 November	Henlow, Beds	Fairey Battle I K7664. 185 Squadron. Struck sports hut on take-off. Pilot & crew safe. 2 civilians killed.
1939		
11 August	Carlton, Beds	Fairey Battle I K9328. 218 Squadron. Struck electricity pylon during exercise flight. Pilot & crew killed.
1940		
21 June	Cranfield, Beds	Miles Master N4767 14 SFTS. Aircraft crashed onto airfield boundary. Crew injured and 3 soldiers killed.
2 July	Cranfield, Beds	Miles Master N7695. 14 SFTS. Aircraft crashed on boundary of airfield during training flight. Pilot killed.

INCIDENT AND ACCIDENT LOG

13 July	Harrold, Beds	Blenheim IV R3597. 218 Squadron. Aircraft crashed at Harrold. Pilot & crew killed.
25 July	Cranfield, Beds	Miles Master N7690 14 SFTS. Aircraft crashed onto airfield during solo training flight. Pilot killed.
28 July	Clop Hill, Beds	Vickers Wellington N3002. 11 OTU. Aircraft crashed at Clop Hill whilst returning to Bassingbourn. Crew safe.
9 August	Cranfield, Beds	Miles Master N7717 14 SFTS. Crashed at RAF Cranfield during training flight. Pilot killed.
20 August	Cranfield, Beds	Oxford I P1834 and P8827. 14 SFTS. Two aircraft collided in mid-air. Both crews killed.
30 August	Luton, Beds	Luftwaffe Air Raid on the town including Vauxhall Plant. 59 killed.
22 September	Luton, Beds	Lone Luftwaffe raider struck Park Street. 9 civilians and 1 serviceman killed.
26 September	Henlow, Beds	Luftwaffe air raid on airfield. 6 killed, 7 injured.
6 October	Colmworth, Beds	Junkers Ju88 Wn.8045. 4/KG30. Shot down by RAF fighters and crashed at Netherstead near Colmworth. 4 killed.
7 October	Turvey, Beds	Oxford I N4729. 14SFTS. Struck a tree and crashed at Newton Park Farm. Pilot & passenger killed.
15 October	Luton, Beds	Luftwaffe air raid on the town. Lone raider hit hat factories in Old Bedford Road. 13 killed & 35 injured.
16 October	Todington, Beds	Wellington X P9276. 9 Squadron. Crashed at Old Park Farm returning from an operation. Pilot killed.
24 October	Eaton Socon, Beds	Dornier 215B Wn.0060. 3/Aufklarungs. Gruppe. Shot down by RAF Hurricanes. Pilot & 2 crew killed, 1 injured.
28 October	Cranfield, Beds	Oxford I N4583. 14 SFTS. Crashed near airfield during solo training flight. Pilot killed.
14 November	Bedford	First Luftwaffe air raid on the town. Two parachute mines dropped.
16 December	Cranfield, Beds	Oxford I N4736. 14 SFTS. Crashed near airfield during solo training flight. Pilot killed.

1941

14 September	Renhold, Beds	Halifax I L9567. 76 Squadron. Crashed at Rectory Farm, Water End, Renhold. Pilot killed, crew baled out.
12 October	Cranfield, Beds	Bristol Blenheim IV L4849. 51 OTU. Crashed in Colmans Orchard, Cranfield. Pilot killed.
19 October	Bedford, Beds	Airacobra I AH852. 601 Squadron. Crashed at Greyfriars Walk. Pilot killed.
15 November	Stanbridge, Beds	Airspeed Oxford L4622. TFPP. Aircraft crashed at Mundays Field, west of Stanbridge. Pilot injured.
5 December	Steppingley, Beds	Bristol Blenheim IV N6172. 51 OTU. Crashed at Beckerings Park, Steppingly. Pilot killed.
24 December	Kempston, Beds	Short Stirling I N6066. 26 Conversion Flight. Aircraft crashed at West End Farm, Kempston. Crew killed.

1942

12 January	Great Staughton	Blenheim I L8661. Crashed on solo training flight. Pilot killed.
27 January	Ampthill, Beds	Blenheim IV N6163. 51 OTU. Crashed at Kingswood on solo training flight. Pilot killed.
12 February	Lidlington, Beds	Boston I AE457. Crashed at North Common Farm during solo training flight. Pilot killed.
1 April	Northill, Beds	Hudson III AE558. 1428 Conversion Flight. Crashed at Grove Farm, Beeston Fields. Crew killed.
6 May	Wootton, Beds	Handley-Page Hampden. 16 OTU. Aircraft crashed at Cook Farm, Wotton. Pilot & crew killed.
30 June	Bedford	Luftwaffe air raid on the town. 4 injured.
6 July	Cranfield, Beds	Havoc I crashed into village on training flight. Pilot & navigator killed, air gunner injured.
23 July	Bedford	Luftwaffe air raid on the town. 14 injured.
30 July	Bedford	Luftwaffe air raid on the town. 8 killed & 61 injured.
12 August	Cranfield, Beds	Havoc I AW409. 51 OTU. Crashed during solo training flight. Pilot killed.
19 August	Ridgmont, Beds	Blenheim I L6623. 51 OTU. Crashed during training flight. Pilot & crew killed.

INCIDENT AND ACCIDENT LOG

31 August	Cranfield, Beds	Blenheim IV N3585. 51 OTU. Crashed at Fensomes Farm during solo training flight. Pilot killed.
22 October	Tempsford, Beds	Whitley V BD228. 161 Squadron, Crashed on returning from Special Duties operation. Pilot killed.
25 October	Clapham, Beds	Havoc BB898. Crashed on first night of night flying training at RAF Twinwoods. Pilot & crew killed.
27 November	Thurleigh, Beds	Havoc I BJ501. 51 OTU. Crashed at Rutters Cottage Meadow on solo training flight. Pilot killed.
5 December	Cranfield, Beds	Beaufighter I R2204. 51 OTU. Pilot injured, navigator killed.
19 December	Gransden, Beds	Stirling I R9265. 149 Squadron. Broke up in mid-air on outward leg of operational flight. Pilot & crew killed.
23 December	Bedford	Two Airacobras of 81st Fighter Group USAAF collided in mid-air and crashed at Miller Road. 3 killed.

1943

15 April	Putnoe, Beds	Beaufighter IF R2098. 415 Fighter Squadron. Crashed on local training flight. USAAF Pilot killed.
15 April	Eaton Ford, Beds	P47-C Thunderbolts 41-6241 & 41-6272 of 78th Fighter Group USAAF collided in mid-air. Both pilots killed.
17 April	Twinwoods, Beds	Beaufighter IF T4646. 51 OTU. Aircraft struck tree on landing. Pilot killed.
16 May	Tempsford, Beds	Lysander R9106. 161 Squadron. Crashed on landing. Pilot killed.
18 July	Turvey, Beds	Mosquito N1014. 1655 MTU. Struck high tension cables & crashed. Norwegian pilot & navigator killed.
7 August	Cranfield, Beds	Whitley BD221 & Oxford LX304 collided in mid-air. Whitley landed safely but Oxford crashed. Crew killed.
23 September	Thurleigh, Beds	B-17F Flying Fortress 42-3449. 306th Bomb Group. Crashed on return from operational flight. 3 crew injured.
9 October	Whipsnade, Beds	P-40E Warhawk 41-35934. 8th AF HQ. Crashed on liaison flight. Pilot killed.
14 October	Riseley, Beds	B-17F Flying Fortress 42-54892 'Cat O'9 Tails'. Crashed in garden after being abandoned. Crew survived.
24 October	Cranfield, Beds	Beaufighter V8230. 51 OTU. Crashed on night training flight. Crew killed.
30 October	Podington, Beds	B-24D Liberator 42-40246 'Thundermug'. 93rd Bomb Group. Crashed on take-off. 2 killed.
11 November	Cranfield, Beds	Dominie I X7368 & Beaufighter IF R2252. 51 OTU. Aircraft collided on approach to airfield. 8 killed.
29 November	Cranfield, Beds	Beaufighter R2249. 51 OTU. Crashed on night training exercise. Pilot killed, navigator Injured.
10 December	Wrestlingworth	P-38H Lightning. 55th Fighter Group. Crashed at Manor Farm following engine failure. Pilot baled out.
19 December	Arlesey, Beds	Halifax II BB364. 138 Special Duties Squadron. Struck chimney at brickworks and crashed. Crew killed.

1944

5 January	Sharnbrook, Beds	B-17F 42-30767. 306th Bomb Group. Crashed on take off from Thurleigh on operational flight. 8 killed.
8 January	Tetworth Hill, Beds	Halifax V LK743. 138 Special Duties Squadron. Crashed on return from aborted operational flight. 8 killed.
23 January	Ridgmont, Beds	Lancaster 1679 Conversion Flight. Pilot & crew killed.
21 February	Shillington, Beds	Lancaster II LL729. 115 Squadron. Crashed on return from operational flight. Pilot & crew killed.
5 March	Tempsford, Beds	Stirling III EE944. 218 Squadron. Crashed on approach to airfield. 5 killed.
13 March	Podington, Beds	P-47C Thunderbolt. 41-6223. Crashed whilst buzzing airfield with another Thunderbolt. Pilot killed.
24 March	Yelden, Beds	B-17G Flying Fortress 42-97578. 305th Bomb Group. Crashed on take off. 18 US personnel & 2 civilians killed.
28 March	Arlesey, Beds	Hudson III FK767. 161 Special Duties Squadron. Crashed on training flight. Pilot & crew killed.
31 March	Cockayne Hatley	Mosquito crashed at Cockayne Hatley. Pilot & crew killed.

2 April	Little Staughton	Undercarriage of RAF Lancaster bomber ripped roof off Baptist Chapel. Crew survived.
26 April	Bletsoe, Beds	B-17G 306th Bomb Group. Crashed after take-off on operational flight. Pilot & crew killed.
7 May	Everton, Beds	Mosquito crashed at Everton. Pilot & crew killed.
9 May	Wilden, Beds	B-17F 306th Bomb Group. Crashed returning from training flight. Pilot & crew survived.
17 May	Great Barford, Beds	Halifax LK736. 138 Special Duties Squadron. Crashed on training flight. Pilot & crew killed.
23 May	Little Staughton.	Avro Anson LT476. 13 OTU. Aircraft attacked by German Raider. Pilot died of wounds. Crew safe.
28 May	Tetworth Hall, Beds	Mosquito crashed at Tetworth Hall. Crew killed. 1 civilian killed and 2 injured.
20 June	Cranfield, Beds	Beaufighter IF X7705. 51 OTU. Crashed on training flight. Pilot killed, navigator baled out.
21 June	Luton, Beds	First V1 to land in Bedfordshire exploded in Ashcroft Road.
28 June	Eaton Socon, Beds	B-24H 42-95321. 801st Bomb Group. Shot down by unknown intruder. Pilot & 2 crew killed. 3 injured.
15 July	Turvey, Beds	B-17 42-31898. 92nd Bomb Group. Crashed at Freers Wood on return from operational flight. 3 killed.
25 July	Turvey, Beds	Tiger Moth BB699. 6 EFTS. Struck HT Cables on training flight and crashed. Pilot & pupil killed.
3 August	Wymington, Beds	B-17G 42-31255. 'Miss Liberty Belle'. 305th Bomb Group. Crashed on return from operational flight. 8 killed.
11 August	Luton, Beds	P-51D Crashed on landing. Pilot survived.
12 August	Penn, Beds	B-17G 'Tomahawk Warrior'. 398th Bomb Group. Crashed on return from operational flight. Pilot & crew killed.
26 August	Old Warden, Beds	Mosquito XVI MM135. 692 Squadron. Crashed on return from operational flight. Pilot & crew killed.
5 September	Eyeworth, Beds	V-1 exploded at Church Farm.
6 October	Thurleigh, Beds	V-1 exploded near Brook Farm.
13 October	Westoning, Beds	V-1 exploded at Horse Hill Farm.
13 October	Maulden, Beds	V-1 exploded at Maulden Wood.
19 October	Potton, Beds	Stirling IV LK207. 161 Special Duties Squadron. Broke up in mid-air during test flight. Pilot & crew killed.
19 October	Little Staughton	Mosquito XVI ML993. 105 Squadron. Crashed at College Farm returning from operational flight. Crew killed.
22 October	Thurleigh, Beds	B-17G 44-38133 WF-F and 43-38030 JJ-E of the 305th Bomb Group collided over Thurleigh. 20 killed.
6 November	Luton, Beds	The first V-2 to strike Bedfordshire landed in Biscot Rd. 19 killed & 196 Injured
16 November	Little Staughton	Mosquito IX ML907. 109 Squadron. Crashed whilst avoiding HT Lines. Pilot & crew killed.
1 December	Cranfield, Beds	Wellington. 1 killed & 1 injured
7 December	Haynes End, Beds	V-2 exploded at local recreation ground.
10 December	Great Barford, Beds	V-1 exploded at Northfield Farm.
10 December	Henlow, Beds	V-1 exploded at Old Runwick Farm. 2 injured.
12 December	Henlow, Beds	V-1 exploded south of Henlow Camp.
18 December	Silsoe, Beds	V-1 exploded by side of A6.
24 December	Podington, Beds	B-17G. 92nd Bomb Group. Crashed at Great Hayes Wood. 7 killed, 3 survived. Alfred Nottage won BEM.

1945

5 January	Gamlingay, Beds	Mosquito XXV KB397. 142 Squadron. Ran out of fuel and made forced landing Hatley Park. Crew killed.
10 January	Arlesey, Beds	V-2 exploded at City Field Farm.
16 January	Biggleswade, Beds	P-51D Mustang 44-14836. 356th Fighter Group. Crashed returning from escort operation. Pilot killed.

29 January	Southill, Beds	Tempest crash landed 400 yards north of Green Man Public House, Stanford. Pilot injured. No Further Details.
5 February	Flitwick, Beds	Typhoon force landed at Wood End. No Further Details.
14 February	Sandy, Beds	Stirling LK236. 161 Squadron & P-51D 42-106448. 364th Fighter Group. Collided in mid-air. 8 killed.
24 February	Flitwick, Beds	Mosquito XVII HK304. 51 OTU. Broke up in mid-air whilst on training flight. Pilot & crew killed.
11 March	Astwood, Beds	P-47M Thunderbolt 44-21125. 56th Fighter Group. Crashed on training flight. Pilot killed.
23 March	Studham, Beds	V-2 exploded at Dagnall Hill.
24 March	Chicksands, Beds	The last V-1 to explode in Bedfordshire struck at Chicksands.
28 April	Cranfield, Beds	Mosquito XII HK129. 51 OTU. Crashed in a snowstorm near the aerodrome. Pilot & crew killed
26 June	Meppershall, Beds	Tempest II MW753. 13 Maintenance Unit. Crashed whilst on a test flight. Pilot killed
18 September	Cockayne Hatley	Liberator GR KN736. 466 Squadron. Crashed whilst on a training flight. 4 killed, 3 injured.

1954

14 July	Cranfield, Beds	Handley-Page Victor HP80 Prototype. WB771. RAE. Crashed on airfield during test flight. Pilot & crew killed.

The grave of 1/Lt William D Sellers, the pilot of the B-17 that crashed on take-off at Yelden.

SOURCES OF INFORMATION

Archives
National Archives
 - Avia Series – Air Accident Investigation Reports
 - Air Series – Station & Operations Record Books
 - FO Series
 - HO Series
The Bedfordshire Records Office
 - Bedfordshire Times
 - Cranfield Burial Registers
Bedfordshire & Luton Archives & Records Service

Websites
55th Fighter Group (www.55th.org)
Air Transport Auxiliary (www.poetryinaction-aviation.com/airtransportauxiliary)
American Battle Monuments Commission (www.abmc.gov)
Ancestry.com (http://www.cwgc.org)
Australian War Memorial (www.awm.gov.au)
Biggleswade Historical Society (http://www.biggleswadehistory.org)
James Frederick Bridge (http://www.xmas.demon.co.uk/genealogy/photoalbumJFB.html)
Canadian Virtual War Memorial (http://www.veterans.gc.ca)
Commonwealth War Graves Commission (http://www.cwgc.org)
Findagrave.com (www.findagrave.com)
Findmypast.com (http://www.findmypast.co.uk)
Footnote.com (www.footnote.com)
London Gazette Archives (http://www.london-gazette.co.uk)
New Zealand Cenotaph Database (www.aucklandmuseum.com)
www.mackz.net
Potton Historical Society (http://www.pottonhistorysociety.com)
www.ww2.com/Forum

My sincere thanks to the following for their assistance;
Debbi Bonas
Julian Evan-Hart
Celia Fulker (Martin-Baker Aircraft Company)
Andrew Gell
Susan Hartline
George Howe (Potton History Society)
Nigel Julian (56th Fighter Group Website)
Simon Parry
Mike Strange (Biggleswade History Society)
Ian White (305th Bomb Group Memorial Association)

REFERENCES

- Anderson, Christopher J. The Men of the Mighty Eighth: The U.S. 8th Air Force, 1942–1945 (2001). London. Greenhill
- Barnes, C.H. Bristol Aircraft Since 1910. (1970). London: Putnam
- Bishop, S & Hey, J. 8th Air Force Losses (Vol.1 – 3.) 1999. Cambridge. Bishop Book Productions
- Boiten, T. Bristol Blenheim. (1998) Marlborough, Wiltshire, UK: The Crowood Press.
- Bowman, Martin. 8th Air Force at War: Memories and Missions, England, 1942–1945. (1994) Cambridge. Patrick Stephens Ltd.
- Bowman, Martin. The Bedford Triangle. (1989) Cambridge. Patrick Stephens Ltd.
- Bowyer, C. Bristol Blenheim. (1984). London: Ian Allan.
- Bowyer, M J. Action Stations 6: Military Airfields of the Cotswolds and Central Midlands. (1989). Cambridge. Patrick Stephens Ltd.
- Chorley, W.R. RAF Bomber Command Losses of the Second World War: Volumes 1-9.(1998) Leicester, UK. Midland Publishing.
- Clark, F. Agents By Moonlight. (1999). Stroud. Tempus Publishing.
- Cull, B. Diver, Diver. (2008). London. Grub Street Publishing.
- Donald, W. John Burn One-Zero-Five. (2005). Peterborough. GMB Publishing.
- Freeman, Roger A. et al. The Mighty Eighth War Diary. (1981). London. Jane's Publishing Company.
- Fry, G L, Eagles Of Duxford. (1991). Shepperton. Ian Allan Publishing.
- Haining, P. The Flying Bomb War. (2002). London: Robson Books.
- Irons, R. Hitler's Terror Weapons: The Price of Vengeance. (2003). New York: HarperCollins Publishers.
- Jefford, C.G. RAF Squadrons. 2nd Edition. (2001) Shrewsbury, UK: Airlife Publishing.
- Mason, Francis K. The British Bomber Since 1914. (1994). London: Putnam Aeronautical Books.
- Maurer, Maurer. Air Force Combat Units of World War II. (1961, republished 1983). Office of Air Force History,
- McLaren, D. Beware The Thunderbolt. (1994). Pennsylvania. Schiffer Publications.
- Merrick, K A. Flights of the Forgotten. (1989). London. Arms & Armour Press
- Miller, Kent D. Fighter Units & Pilots of the 8th Air Force September 1942 – May 1945. (2000). Pennsylvania: Schiffer Publishing.
- O'Neil, B D. Half a Wing, Three Engines & a Prayer. (1999). Washington. McGraw-Hill Publishing.
- Ramsay, W. The Blitz Then & Now (Volume 3). (1990). London: Battle of Britain Prints International.
- Sharman, S. Sir Martin Baker. 1996. Yeovil. Patrick Stephens Publishing.
- Zaloga, S. V-1 Flying Bomb 1942–52. (2005). Oxford, UK: Osprey Publishing.